Good Homes magazine

101 BATHROOMS

STYLISH ROOM SOLUTIONS

Julie Savill

BBC BOOKS

CONTENTS

BUDGET 126

CLASSIC 146

CREATIVE 188

INTRODUCTION

There's something very indulgent and slightly decadent about the thought of going all out for your dream bathroom. But this workhorse room is on duty 24 hours a day, working even harder than the kitchen and used by virtually every visitor to your home – so doesn't it deserve a bit of glamour and stardust?

Your plans for your bathroom are likely to be dictated by space as much as budget. Older properties, originally built with an outside loo, have occasionally sacrificed a bedroom to create a luxuriously large bathing space with, in the most extravagant cases, room for a sofa or chaise longue. But for most of us that is a little fantasy to save for another day while we battle with more recent homes, bathrooms of more petite proportions and all the demands of a busy family.

A white suite is your best friend in the bathroom. It's timeless, looks a treat with all manner of colour schemes and won't put off prospective purchasers if you decide to sell up and move on. Of course, if money is very tight or you are doing a quick fix before putting the place on the market, there are ways to bring a coloured suite more up to date – you'll find some ideas in this book. If, on the other hand, you have a little more cash to splash, your first move should be to ditch the avocado or primrose yellow in favour of a little white or palest cream number.

A daring raid on a few bathroom showrooms is your next move. Arm yourself with a whole range of brochures – not only for the bathrooms illustrated, but for the neat little sets of graph paper and cut-out templates for loos, basins and baths you'll find at the back. A happy evening spent with scissors and one of these planning kits will let you explore all the possibilities before taking the plunge and ordering your new fittings.

Once you've made your plans and your plumber has the major fittings in place, the really creative stuff starts. Forget wall to wall white tiles – a bathroom is as deserving as any other room in the house of a carefully considered and thoughtfully executed colour scheme. Consider how the room is going to be used for the practical elements. If you have young children, water-proof walls and floors are going to be a top priority but don't leave yourself out of the equation. As well as the pure function of keeping everyone clean, the bathroom may be the only room where you can lock the door and be truly alone for half an hour. Make sure it has flexible lighting, plenty of storage to clear the clutter and somewhere to rest a glass of wine. At the end of a hard day, this is your sanc-tuary and you'll thank yourself for the little extras you've managed to plan in…

Julie Savill, Editor
BBC Good Homes magazine

The look: Form and colour fall into perfect harmony when lush lilac creates a chic setting for shapely fittings. The sensual curves of the suite offset the geometric wall stripes and the angular lines of the bath surround.

Colour: Cool and contemporary, purple and lilac are rich in colour but also relaxing to live with, and team beautifully with white and chrome fittings. This calming scheme blends a range of toning shades – from pale lavender floor tiles to deep purple accents. Contrasting wall treatments highlight the room's unusual shape, with light stripes livening up the foreground walls and a more intense lilac creating a cosier feel in the bathing area.

Suite: The suite combines minimalist styling with smooth curves for a contemporary, contoured look that's easy on the eye. The gently rounded shape of the basin is echoed by the close-coupled loo. The corner bath also adds attractive shape, giving a more individual look than a standard rectangular design. Sleek chrome taps highlight the suite's modern appeal.

Walls: If you want to add interest to walls without overpowering your room with pattern, paint stripes in two similar shades. Or, for an even subtler effect, alternate gloss and matt emulsion in the same hue, creating a variation in texture. Broad horizontal stripes will make a room feel wider but also appear to lower the ceiling, so are best used in tall rooms.

Floor: Ceramic tiles make a hardwearing bathroom floor and are available in many colours. However, they feel chilly beneath bare feet and can be slippery when wet. You may also find it difficult to keep the grout clean.

The look: Cool cream paint and tiles the colour of milky coffee give this bathroom a tranquil atmosphere, perfect for enjoying a long soak. Tongue-and-groove boarding encloses the bath and loo cistern, giving the small space a streamlined look.

Colour: If you want to enhance the illusion of space in a small room, pale colours are your best bet. White is an especially effective brightener but can feel stark and chilly; soft cream is much easier to warm to and creates a light but relaxing environment. Using the same shade throughout a room also makes it feel bigger, as it avoids breaking up the wall area with different colours. Cream paint covers both the walls and tongue-and-groove panelling, and coffee-coloured tiles in a closely toning shade continue the visual harmony. The wooden flooring and Venetian blind add a hint of warm,

natural colour to complement and offset the pale neutrals.

Suite: Wall-mounted basins are available in smaller sizes than pedestal designs but must be fixed to a solid wall that can take the weight of the basin when full of water. Here an H-shaped structure, made from timber and roughly plastered plasterboard, provides additional support. Back-to-wall loos have a cistern that can be concealed behind a false wall or panelling, and boxing this one in with tongue and groove that matches the bath panels gives a neat, uniform look.

Window: A Venetian blind is a versatile treatment for a small or narrow window as its adjustable slats give you complete control over light and privacy levels. Wooden blinds are now widely available, and work well in a contemporary setting.

The look: Orange is a warm, 'advancing' colour that creates a welcoming atmosphere. This room intensifies its rich, glowing quality by using toning shades repeatedly in different fittings and materials.

Colour: Strong colour looks at home in smaller spaces if similar shades are used over most available surfaces. The bathroom is the perfect place to experiment with colour from all types of materials, and here copper, brass, lacquered wood and plastic all add a new dimension to the palette of fiery hues. Different textures also affect colour – glossy surfaces reflect light, helping to enhance the illusion of space, while brushed or satin finishes provide a contrast for matt walls without the need to add different colours.

Basin unit: A compact basin fitted into a narrow washstand is a neat solution for a small bathroom, and shelves provide easily accessible storage. The wooden cabinet is dressed to fit the scheme with a covering of thin copper sheeting, available from metal merchants or large DIY stores, which is also used to make a reflective splash-back. The matching towel rail is made from 22mm copper piping, with elbows at either end. A tall-spout mixer tap with gleaming brass finish completes the line-up of glamorous metallics.

Bath: Save strong shades for walls and accessories – white fittings are more versatile than coloured ones. An edging of triangular ceramic tiles in oxblood red helps to incorporate the bath into the scheme.

Accessories: The yellow stool and brown towels add dashes of accent colour that help to offset the hot reds and oranges. The round mirror, complete with candle sconces, enhances the room's cosy, romantic atmosphere.

BATHROOM TIP
Good ventilation is vital in a bathroom, especially if it has no window. An extractor fan fitted to an outside wall will reduce condensation. A fan can be set to come on with the light and continue working for a while after it is switched off

The look: Simple wooden cabinets and elegantly styled sanitaryware bring Shaker style into the bathroom, with natural textures and traditional accessories bringing out the essence of all-American country charm.

Colour: Pale neutrals offset by warm wood tones create a look that's plain but inviting. The richness of the cream used on the units is enhanced by contrast with the white walls and fittings. The natural browns of the woods stand out against the light backdrop and make their presence felt by appearing throughout the room. The horizontal lines of the peg rail and countertop are echoed by the wood-effect laminate flooring.

Suite: In keeping with Shaker principles, the fittings appear stylish but functional, the basin and bath combining distinctive form with generous capacity. The swan-neck taps have an old-fashioned, utilitarian feel that is also well in character. Some bathroom companies can design and install a combination of sanitaryware and furniture, so that fittings can be incorporated into your storage system. The back-to-wall loo has its cistern hidden inside the cupboards, and the semi-recessed basin is built into the countertop, allowing space below to be used for plenty of storage.

Storage: Fitted units are the neatest way of maximizing storage capacity, and an L-shaped layout makes efficient use of space. The doors of the base cabinets have classic Shaker styling, with simple recessed panels. Their smart chrome handles echo the taps. The wall cabinet adds further concealed storage. It also has attractive display niches at either side, and doors that double as mirrors. Shaker traditions continue with the peg rail and selection of oval wooden boxes, both hallmarks of the style.

CONTEMPORARY

The look: Simple modern fittings show off their curvaceous lines against a restful backdrop of deep blue and taupe, while accessories add a hint of oriental style to complement this coolly minimalist scheme.

Colour: Painting neighbouring walls in contrasting colours can add an extra dimension to a room. For a calming effect, choose two shades that are similar in tone. Neutrals are a safe bet as they team well with most other colours, and cool hues such as blue have a more relaxing effect than reds, yellows and oranges. This cool combination is complemented by the warmer natural tones of the wood flooring, and freshened by the white fittings and the pale colours of the painting on the wall.

Suite: The sanitaryware combines style with practicality, the compact floorstanding loo featuring a streamlined upright cistern and the bowl of the circular basin offering a large capacity without taking up too much space. The chrome-plated monobloc taps with traditional controls would suit either a modern or classic setting.

Glass wall: Glass blocks make ideal partitions for modern bathrooms. As well as having an up-to-the-minute feel, they provide just enough privacy to screen a bath or shower area without blocking out natural light. You can buy them from DIY stores, but it's best to get a professional to lay them as glass walls must be reinforced for safety.

Accessories: The slatted wooden bench, waffle-weave towels and shapely dark vase add a suggestion of oriental minimalism. Every room benefits from a touch of art, and the bathroom is no exception: the painted canvas echoes the wall colours, bringing them together as subtler shades.

BATHROOM TIP
When planning a new bathroom layout, take into account the position of existing plumbing – it can be costly to change. If possible, the loo and bidet should be placed side by side

16

The look: Although based on the colours of nature, this is no twee country-style bathroom. Alluring dark woods and subtle shades of stone create a sophisticated backdrop for modernist fittings. Used as simple blocks of colour, they combine minimalist styling with natural warmth.

Colour: The palette of restrained neutrals reflects the contrasting light and dark shades found in nature. The pale beige flooring and the grey paintwork on the right-hand wall blend with soft cream and white, while the deeper shades of the stone-coloured tiling and dark wood surfaces give the scheme a stronger look. Dark woods suggest oriental or jungle inspiration: to bring out that exotic quality, add accessories in jazzier accent colours, such as bright red and leaf green.

Suite: Clean curves and simple design give the fittings their thoroughly contemporary character. The freestanding bath creates an air of luxury, its oval shape and generous proportions making it the focal point of the room. It is sold complete with the wooden feet that fit in so well with this natural scheme. The chrome taps have gold-plated controls, a distinctive detail that adds a hint of glamour. They are fitted centrally so that two people can share the tub in comfort.

Accessories: The large mirror that spans the width of the far wall helps to give the room a greater sensation of space. To maintain minimalist purity, there are only a few toiletries and vases on display – these reflect the browns and creams of the scheme. A small slatted stool reinforces the look with further natural texture.

The look: Mix old and new for a bathroom full of colour and character. An original roll-top bath complements this high-ceilinged Victorian room, but striking colour contrasts and slick storage create a look that's bang up to date.

Colour: Clean up with dazzling white for a bright, modern atmosphere – white flooring and wall tiles are guaranteed to lighten the mood. Teaming them with deep blue forms a dramatic contrast, adding real colour impact. Accents of fuchsia pink help to soften the look, and using this colour to paint the bath makes it seem at home in the contemporary scheme.

Suite: A traditionally styled bath/shower mixer with a chrome finish is in character with the classic roll-top bath. The basin, loo and bidet have clean, simple lines that suit the modern scheme, but their smooth curves also complement those of the bath.

Storage: With a radiator running along most of one wall, the room had little space for freestanding storage furniture. The solution was a clever system, built by a local carpenter, which fits around and above the radiator and incorporates open shelves, mirrored wall cabinets and a peg rail. Positioning the rail above the radiator ensures that towels hung from it remain warm, aired and dry.

Floor: Many old houses still have original floorboards which, if in good condition, can be painted. Two coats of white floor paint give these boards a hard-wearing finish. Bathroom floors must be sealed with varnish to stop water penetrating the wood.

The look: With billowing curtains and blue-washed walls, this room borrows the colours of a spring sky to create a beautifully refreshing atmosphere. Natural textures and accessories join a varied mix of furniture and fittings to give the look its laid-back, modern charm.

Colour: In a room where daylight floods in through a tall window, the pale blue and white scheme guarantees an ultra-bright environment. The checks of the mosaic tiling, shower curtain and cushion cover vary the tone with hints of darker blue, which are reinforced by the ultramarine border painted around the floor. The natural tones and textures of the pine flooring and loo seat provide a warm contrast for the airy colours.

Walls: Applying paint as a colourwash adds interest to large wall areas, and pale shades create a cloudy, ethereal effect. First apply a base coat of white paint and leave to dry. Then either dilute your top colour with water until you get the strength you want, or mix in a little scumble glaze. Working on a small area at a time, use large brush strokes to spread the colour over the wall, allowing some of the white base coat to show through.

Suite: The reproduction claw-foot bath fits in well with the room's Victorian features, and the basin has classic lines. Laid-back looks thrive on a mix of styles, so the bath and basin sit happily amid the room's fresh, contemporary decor.

Accessories: A sheer white curtain screens the large window while letting plenty of light filter through. Plants, pebbles and a fibre mat all contribute natural texture, while the Lloyd Loom chair adds both character and comfort.

The look: Modern minimalism demands clutter-free surfaces and clean lines, and this room's fitted units make both possible. The beautifully rounded suite and light but livable colour scheme give cutting-edge looks a gentler complexion.

Colour: Although white is the most versatile choice for a suite, cream creates a softer look, and is complemented by walls and flooring in a similar shade. The storage units mellow the scheme further with the natural look of wood, but their black countertops add smart definition. The lime green wall also sharpens things up with a dash of fresh, contemporary colour.

Suite: The organic shapes of the fittings provide a stylish contrast for the straight lines of the storage units. These practical units keep the room streamlined by concealing the cistern and pipes of the back-to-wall loo, as well as the pipework to the semi-recessed basin. The double-ended bath has a central tap control, a sleek single-lever mixer in shiny chrome.

Storage: Bathrooms generate a surprising amount of clutter – toiletries, towels, cleaning materials – much of which is not worth keeping on show. Fitted units look neat and modern, while providing particularly generous storage capacity. A combination of drawers and cupboards takes care of different-sized items, while the countertops and the glass shelves above the basin provide display space for dressier accessories.

Shower room: If you have the space and resources to build one, a shower room will provide total privacy for showering. To save space, choose sliding doors or ones that open into the cubicle, as these do not take up additional floor area.

The look: If you haven't space for a bath, look on the bright side – showers use less water, which is reflected in your fuel bills. An open-plan shower area maintains the illusion of light and space in this narrow room.

Colour: While off-white tiles keep the look bright and airy, the overall colour palette achieves a relaxing atmosphere, combining soft green with pale neutrals. A few grey tiles and a grey marble shelf on the partition wall add subtle interest to the shower area, while accents of wood and wicker add touches of welcome warmth.

Shower: If you can give your shower enough space, you may not need to enclose it completely, but make sure the surrounding walls have a splashproof covering, such as tiles. Here a low wall protects the loo and basin from the shower's spray. A shower head on a sliding rail, with a detachable handset, gives greater flexibility than a fixed design. The head can be adjusted to suit people of different heights, or removed from its fitting for hair-washing or cleaning the shower space.

Suite: The smooth curves of the loo and basin provide a contrast of form with the geometric lines of the shower area and tiling. The loo is a close-coupled design, which looks neater than a model where the cistern and bowl are linked by a connecting pipe.

Accessories: Bath mats are essential in a carpeted room; two large ones catch splashes. A trendy wire basket on the shower wall and a glass shelf above the basin keep washing items handy. The wicker laundry basket and wooden picture frames add a hint of country style to this contemporary scheme.

The look: Create a dazzling contrast with crisp white and brilliant azure blue. The strength of the white fittings against the dark backdrop is the key to this vibrant look.

Colour: For maximum effect, be brave with your background colour – choose a deep, intense blue and use it to cover the walls. The fittings will sing out against it, but adding a panel of white tiles increases their impact, creating a more equal balance with the blue. Add texture to soften the look, with green mosaic-effect floor tiles and a scattering of mottled lime tiles to break up the plain white splashback. The dark wood and wicker cabinet introduces warmth, and green glass accessories add drama as their colour is intensified by the blue walls.

Suite: Fittings with clean, simple designs reinforce the bold modern appeal of the look, offering no fussy details to distract from the colour contrast. The chrome mixer taps also have streamlined contemporary looks, with easy-to-operate lever controls. The bath is panelled with three strips of MDF, painted with a white satin finish.

Floor: The flooring looks like ceramic tiles but is in fact a high-quality vinyl, which is warmer and softer underfoot. Waterproof and easy to clean, vinyl designs include a wide range of patterns that look just like real stone, wood or ceramics, including these convincing mosaic-effect tiles.

Furniture and accessories: The garden chair and the natural textures of the storage cabinet add character to the look. Rope pots displayed on the simple shelf introduce further woven texture, while the glitzy mosaic border of the mirror echoes the floor tiles.

BATHROOM TIP
Monobloc basin mixer taps fit into a single hole, leaving more of your basin top free for toiletries or accessories. By enabling you to mix hot water with cold before it leaves the spout, they reduce the risk of scalding

CONTEMPORARY

The look: Curvy lines manipulate space in this tiny bathroom, adding interest among the simple styling and understated colour scheme, and softening the overall look.

Colour: The grey wall tiles are pale enough not to overpower the small space, while providing a tranquil backdrop for the white fittings. In this super-subtle scheme, the horizontal band of blue provides welcome colour interest, and also breaks up the wall area, helping to make the room appear wider.

Walls: A surround built out from the left-hand wall follows the lines of the bath and provides a screen between the shower area and basin. Its curvy walls are made from waterproof plywood covered with mosaic tiles, and recesses knocked into the ply provide useful storage niches. If you've never worked with mosaic, don't imagine that the tiles must be stuck on one by one.

They can be bought attached to backing sheets, which makes it easy to apply blocks of them to large areas. Each sheet is glued on tile-side down, then the backing paper is peeled away when the adhesive is dry.

Suite: A curved or corner bath could be a good idea if your bathroom is an awkward shape. Although it occupies a similar floor area to a standard rectangular bath, it may allow space in areas where you need it – to allow room to open a door, for example. The deep basin has a traditional farmhouse style, and the simple plywood surround suits its utilitarian character.

BATHROOM TIP
Frosted or sandblasted glass ensures privacy. Give clear window or door panes a similar effect by applying glass etch spray, available from DIY stores. Mask off surrounding areas, then spray on several light coats

30

The look: With looks that could have come straight from a Manhattan apartment, this spacious room contrasts dark stone flooring with white walls and fittings to create a bold, modernist scheme.

Colour: The strong contrast lends impact to an essentially simple scheme, where light and dark shades are balanced in equal quantities. The pale grey mosaic tiling around the bath almost blends with the white, offering a subtle variation in tone to soften its starkness. The blue wall lifts the look with a dash of cool colour.

Suite: Earning their place in this strikingly modern setting, the fittings have no fussy details to disturb their rounded curves and clean lines, although the bow-fronted bath gets a subtle touch of interest from the strip of pale grey highlighting its curved edge. The contemporary loo has a neat, compact design, while the sink's pedestal basin boasts a bowl of generous proportions. Chrome-plated mixer taps complete the sleek up-to-date styling.

Floor: Real stone flooring has natural beauty and is extremely hardwearing, but is also expensive and can feel cold underfoot. If you want a cheaper alternative, vinyl designs include many good stone lookalikes that will leave more cash in your pocket and are cosier for bare feet.

Accessories: In a space where the flooring dominates, a tall narrow mirror above the basin acts as a visual device to draw the eye upwards, adding vertical interest to the room and impact to the blue wall. The blue is repeated behind the circular cutouts of the eye-catching contemporary artwork, which add a spot of bold but lively pattern to the plain scheme.

The look: This ultra-minimalist shower room uses all the tricks of form and design to create a beautifully spacious feel. Wall-mounted fittings are the epitome of modern simplicity, while reflective materials and pale colours capitalize on light streaming through the large skylight windows.

Colour: The white walls and ceiling maximize the feeling of space, and pale beige flooring keeps the look light while softening the overall effect. Continuing the tiling onto the walls of the shower area and the housing behind the fittings creates a seamless look, enhancing the room's streamlined feel. The glass screen adds colour while reflecting light, its cool aqua offset by the warm tan accents of the wooden window frames.

Suite: Wall-mounted fittings are perfect for pared-down looks. Smart and simple, all their workings, such as cisterns and pipes, can be concealed behind a false wall. With the floor area left free, they also make cleaning easier.

Shower screen: Keeping things simple is the key to minimalist design, and a plain glass partition screens off the shower area as effectively as a fancy enclosure. Make sure you use safety glass that complies with BS6206.

Windows: If you have a dingy bathroom that lies directly beneath a roof, skylight windows could help to lift the gloom. As they don't take up valuable wall space, you can make them as large as possible to flood the room with light. Another advantage is that they don't present privacy problems, so won't need dressing – unless, of course, you are overlooked by a high-rise building!

BATHROOM TIP
Towel rails linked to your heating system will not work in summer when it is turned off. If you want warm towels all year round, choose a rail connected to your hot water system, or one that is powered by an electric element

The look: Clean lines and clever storage have turned this small bathroom into a minimalist haven. Although it measures just 1.7 x 2.1m, clearing out clutter and other furniture has allowed space for a generously sized bath and a chunky basin.

Colour: All-white walls maximize the illusion of space and light in a tiny room, and using the same mosaic tiles on both walls and floor creates a seamless appearance. However, a white room needn't be a dull one. Liven things up with bold blocks of colour – lime green covers the bath panelling, and the cabinet above the loo is painted a rich magenta. Bright accessories, such as the bath mat, also add impact, while the silver shower curtain instils an air of contemporary glamour.

Suite: The sanitaryware has a streamlined look, thanks to an ingenious false wall, which conceals a spaghetti of pipework. The back-to-wall loo has its cistern attached to the real wall, but the false wall built over it leaves only the toilet bowl and handle visible. The components of the suite are all from different ranges: the compact loo is teamed with a large, traditional-shaped basin and a roomy bath. The basin's trendy pillar tap, designed by Philippe Starck, enhances the room's modern appeal.

Storage: Unobtrusive storage keeps clutter out of sight. The bath panels are hinged doors, which open to allow cleaning materials to be stashed behind them. Above the loo, a broad but shallow cupboard with shelves inside provides space for toiletries.

BATHROOM TIP
If your bathroom is shared by children or elderly people, make sure it is safe and user-friendly for them. Helpful features include non-slip flooring or mats, easy-to-operate tap controls and grab rails beside the bath

The look: The powerful contrast between deep purple and bright yellow makes an enlivening colour statement in this room, bringing a suite with classic styling bang up to date.

Colour: This scheme shows how complementary colours – any two that lie directly opposite each other on the colour wheel – can bring out the best in each other, forming a vibrant contrast rather than a nasty clash. When combining two strong colours, keep the deeper one for the lower part of the room. It 'grounds' the scheme, while the brighter shade keeps the atmosphere light and airy. Take the wall colours over shelves and skirtings for continuity.

Wood panelling: A bathroom without tiles knocks pounds off the budget. If you've moved the suite and damaged the walls, tongue-and-groove panelling is a quick cover-up; here it has been taken up to shoulder height and topped with a narrow shelf. Widely available from DIY stores, the boards are easy to fit and can be painted any colour you like. Apply matt varnish after painting to protect them from damp.

Suite: Sanitaryware with a classic shape is ideal if you have modern tastes but live in an older house. It is complemented by traditional-style pillar taps and a dark wood loo seat. Surrounding the bath with panelling that matches the walls allows the purple to make greater impact.

Accessories: A scheme of two bold colours needs touches of a third for balance, so accessories introduce flashes of sharp green. A beaded curtain is a lighthearted touch at the window. For extra privacy, hang a roller blind behind it or cover the window with etching spray, which gives the look of frosted glass.

The look: With the sleek simplicity of city style, this room combines a smart palette of greys and black with the fashionable glimmer of glass and silver. Compact contemporary fittings soften the look with their graceful curves.

Colour: Unassuming greys give the room a relaxing feel; using different shades on the two walls adds interest to the overall effect. Black floor tiles drive home the smartness of the scheme, providing a bold contrast with the white skirtings and fittings. The sparkle of silver and glass accessories adds high-tech glamour.

Suite: The sculptural shapes of the fittings contrast with the straight lines of the walls, window and accessories, while their compact design enhances the room's modernist appeal. The close-coupled loo has a slimline cistern with neat push-button flush, and a pan that features smooth curves for easy cleaning. The semi-pedestal design of the trendy wall-hung basin leaves no messy pipework on display, and its monobloc tap with single lever control also has an unfussy modern look. A narrow strip of aqua-coloured glass, fixed to the wall with three screws, makes a stylish splashback.

Lighting: As well as a background light source, bathrooms need efficient illumination near mirrors to provide good light for close-up tasks such as shaving or applying make-up. These vertical lamps echo the shape of the tall mirror and add glowing yellow accents to warm up the scheme.

Accessories: The geometric arrangement of mirror, glass shelves and lamps creates an attractive wall feature. The stylish laundry basket echoes the silvery sheen of the tap and freestanding chrome towel rail, while fresh flowers displayed in a black and silver vase add a further touch of luxury.

BATHROOM TIP
To save water, choose a loo cistern that offers a choice of flushing modes. A dual control allows you to opt for a shorter flush when a longer burst of water is not necessary

CONTEMPORARY

The look: Blue and white is a popular colour scheme for a bathroom, but original design ideas, such as the textured wall and extended bath surround, lift this one out of the ordinary.

Colour: The contrast between blue and white creates a fresh, invigorating feel. A textured, rough-plaster effect softens the austerity of the white walls, while the woodgrain of the bath surround and the woodstain effect of the flooring add a natural dimension to the deep blues. The colourful mosaic tiles, in a medley of blues and aquas, add pattern and pace to the scheme.

Bath: Boxing in the bath with a surround that continues beyond its end not only adds a stylish feature to the room but also creates a handy ledge that can be used for sitting on after a bath and as a display area for toiletries or plants. The surround is constructed from timber, and the sides are painted with a blue woodstain. Mosaic tiles create a fashionable, wipe-clean surface for the top.

Walls: The rough wall finish is created by mixing powdered tile adhesive into a thick paste and applying it with spreaders. To get a patterned effect, press a rubber doormat or other textured surface into the paste before it dries to imprint the design. Paint in the colour of your choice, then add a coat of clear acrylic varnish for a damp-resistant finish.

Floor: The floor is covered in trendy blue laminate planks, with strips of darker blue inserted at an angle to add interest. Their woodstain effect matches the finish on the side of the bath surround, and a wooden duckboard makes a coordinating bath mat.

CONTEMPORARY

The look: Clean up with white walls, flooring and fittings for a sparkling modern scheme. Bands of mint and aqua tiles add subtle colour while keeping the look as refreshing as a toothpaste ad.

Colour: There's nothing like white for clearing out the cobwebs and replacing them with a spotless environment. Using white throughout will defeat dinginess in a small room and make a large space dazzlingly bright. Inject a dash of colour to lift its clinical feel though – soft shades of mint and aqua are complemented by deeper turquoise accents in the towels and glass vase.

Suite: Compact sanitaryware with smooth curves is perfectly compatible with the pristine contemporary decor. Wall-mounted pieces, such as the basin, have an especially neat look, and allow for easy cleaning of the floor area

below. Gleaming chrome adds high-tech shine and coordinates all the details in the room, from the taps and toothbrush holder to the trim surrounding the glass door of the shower cubicle.

Tiles: Using tiles to cover both the walls and floor makes for an easy-clean bathroom. They can look monotonous, but the bands of coloured tiles break up the high walls, their subtle sponged effect providing additional interest. Using brick-shaped tiles on the floor also varies the effect a little.

Window: A sheer roller blind in a pale aqua provides both privacy and colour without blocking out light. Roller blinds are available in a range of sizes, or you can make one by using your own fabric and buying the fittings separately. These are sold in kits, and you can cut the roller to fit the width of your window.

BATHROOM TIP
For truly clean looks, keep your sanitaryware free of limescale. To remove it, apply a mixture of equal parts of hot vinegar and salt using a toothbrush, and leave until it can be scrubbed off

The look: An up-to-the-minute colour scheme, concealed storage, and fittings that combine designer looks with the latest technology mean this room scores highly on both form and function.

Colour: Aqua walls and white tiles make a refreshing combination, and sleek metallic fittings and accessories enhance its cool, modern appeal. The tan bath panelling and basin unit add a hint of warmth, while the rubber flooring grounds the scheme with a deeper shade of blue.

Suite: A double-ended bath with smart central filler and plug means no more debates about who sits at the tap end! This bath also has thermostatic settings that allow water to be set at a specific temperature. The round basin unit is another state-of-the-art design that fits neatly into a corner. Its semi-concealed shelving keeps toiletries tidily hidden but close at hand.

Storage: Flat MDF doors make an unobtrusive frontage for cupboards set into the space above the basin. Painted in a mix of colours, they are also drilled with holes so lights fitted inside can shine through. The door directly over the basin doubles as a surface for a mirror. More cupboard space is included in the triangular structure beside the bath.

Towel rail: A heated rail keeps towels toasty. If you want it to heat the room too, choose one that includes a radiator function as others won't provide enough warmth. It can be mounted high on the wall to save space – just make sure everyone can reach the towels.

BATHROOM TIP
Be aware of safety when planning your lighting. Electricity plus water equals danger, so make sure any fittings you buy are suitable for bathrooms. Lights should be turned on using a pull cord or a switch outside the room

CONTEMPORARY

The look: Get the elements of urban chic with cool colours, innovative designs and reflective materials, such as glass and chrome, all brought together in a minimalist scheme.

Colour: Refreshing colours and pale woods ensure a bright, modern feel. Light from the overhead window glances off white walls and smooth wood flooring, while aqua-coloured tiling gives the shower enclosure a more inviting atmosphere. The walls are covered mostly in glass mosaics, but borders of standard-sized turquoise tiles help to link the white and aqua areas. Scarlet towels bring the scheme to life with splashes of hot colour.

Shower: If you don't want to fit a bath, then make the most of your shower by surrounding it with a spacious walk-in enclosure. This gives you plenty of room to move around, and means that two people can share a shower comfortably. Clear glass walls help to maintain the illusion of space, and even increase it by reflecting light. A DIY alternative would be to build a glass brick cubicle.

Basin: Many small basins feature state-of-the-art shapes, colours and materials. Providing a stylish focal point at the far end of the room, this simple curved bowl made from aqua-coloured glass sits in a freestanding unit that provides counter space on either side. Taps are mounted on the wall above.

Accessories: The large round mirror echoes the curves of the basin bowl and unit, boosting its decorative effect. In the corner below, a discreet chrome rack keeps toiletries under control, saving them from cluttering the countertop.

The look: Crisp and clean, this scheme combines polished metal and pristine white for the purest take on bathroom style. Pale blue walls complement the cool, clinical mood, while a dose of bright red helps to energize the look.

Colour: Fittings and furniture with white or metallic finishes ensure a modern, high-tech feel, but medical chic needs a dash of colour to make it livable. A fresh mid-tone shade of blue is sufficiently intense to give the room a more intimate feel, but also looks cool and clean. Painting the upper part of the walls in a lighter shade maintains the airy atmosphere. The towels bring the blues to life with warmer colours and stimulating stripes, while accents of black in the mosaic tiles and mirror frame add depth to the pale scheme.

Suite and furniture: You don't have to buy a matching suite – combine pieces from different ranges to suit your needs. If you can manage without a full-size wash basin, a tiny sink like this one will fit easily into the smallest bathroom. Use the space you save to slot in a generous storage cabinet, which includes closed cupboards to help you keep the room clutter-free. Metal surfaces not only suit this look but also earn their keep in small spaces by bouncing light around. The bath is boxed in with plywood covered with panels of stainless steel.

Accessories: Chrome accessories add further metallic shine, the tall ladder making a striking towel rail. The white shower curtain is made from kite fabric, which is cheap to buy.

BATHROOM TIP
If bath oils leave greasy marks on metal surfaces, wipe them away using methylated spirit

The look: Form follows function in this cutting-edge bathroom. The basin and loo are by celebrated designer Philippe Starck, and a superbly simple Italian bath takes centre stage.

Colour: A blend of pale blues and greys creates a sophisticated backdrop for state-of-the-art fittings, the soft smoky shade on the walls harmonizing with the iridescent greeny-grey of the floor tiles. Mirror-like metallics enhance the air of high-tech chic, while wood surfaces introduce a touch of warmth to make the cool scheme feel more friendly. Towels add subtle accent colours of muted jade, lilac and cream.

Suite: Shape is an important element of style, especially where bathroom suites are concerned. With their combination of straight lines and flowing modern curves, these fittings epitomize 21st-century cool. The close-coupled floorstanding loo has a wonderfully slimline cistern, and the bowl shares the distinctive conical shaping of the bidet and freestanding basin unit. Placing the generously sized bath in the centre of the room, and at an angle, shows off its shape to advantage and turns it into a focal point.

Storage: A gleaming chrome cabinet on wheels provides high-style storage, and can be moved wherever it's needed. The small wooden drawer unit attached to the mirror base is handy for stashing small items, such as cosmetics, while a simple wall-mounted shelf keeps everyday essentials within reach.

Floor: Laminate sheet flooring that resembles glass mosaic squares is perfect for a chic, contemporary scheme. Although rather pricey as laminates go, it's a worthwhile investment, combining the iridescent shimmer and reflective qualities of real glass with a practical, hardwearing surface.

The look: Deep turquoise and watery aquas create a feeling of well-being and harmony. Team them with a mix of traditional fittings and modern furniture for an intensely relaxing bathroom.

Colour: A combination of closely toning shades creates a look that has visual interest yet, with no strong contrasts to jar the eye, exudes a wonderfully calming mood. This room uses blocks of soft blue and aqua on the walls, and juxtaposes floor tiles of similar harmonious shades. White fittings and woodwork, plus the punchier turquoise of the bath and splashback, give the look a more upbeat feel.

Suite: If you want a bathroom that encourages you to pamper yourself, generously proportioned traditional fittings will add an air of luxury to the most modern setting. A freestanding roll-top bath with elaborate claw feet makes an inviting centrepiece, and blends in perfectly when painted in the room's colours. The large basin also has a commanding presence, with angular mouldings and classic-style taps. A neat splashback of toughened glass offsets its traditional looks.

Furniture: The shelf unit and director's chair reassert the modern feel created by the cool blues. The sleek chrome shelving adds a high-tech glimmer, and provides display space for colourful accessories. The wooden chair introduces a more casual note, while enhancing the air of comfort.

Floor: Choosing flooring in a similar colour to the walls ensures a relaxing atmosphere, and if you opt for ceramic tiles you're sure to find shades to match. There is an enormous range available, and they make a relatively inexpensive floorcovering. Try using colours to create interesting effects – here two tones arranged in barely perceptible stripes create a subtle watery look.

The look: Unfussy design works best in small spaces, but they needn't miss out on character. This shower room gives contemporary simplicity a Victorian twist. Reproduction taps and a bathhouse-style floor evoke the 19th-century feel, while glass shelving and 'dressing-room' lighting bring the look bang up to date.

Colour: A combination of black, white and cream is a smart but simple choice for this tiny room. The cream-coloured walls have a space-enhancing effect but give a softer, more traditional look than pure white. Using two different kinds of tiles adds interest – those on the lower wall have a more textured, glazed finish than the flat, matt ones above – and separating them with a line of dark blue pencil tiles gives the impression of a Victorian dado rail. Against this restrained backdrop, the chequerboard flooring makes a strong style statement, its boldly contrasting black and white tiles adding impact as well as character to the room.

Suite: The clean, contemporary lines of the basin and loo keep the overall look simple, their smooth curves contrasting with the geometric checks of the flooring. However, the old-fashioned pillar taps enhance the Victorian feel, showing how important details can be in adding style to a room.

Shower: If you opt for a shower instead of a bath, choose a large enclosure to give it a more luxurious feel. A glass door will prevent it from making your room feel cramped – choose one that opens inwards to save space.

Accessories: A sleek chrome bin and a slim glass shelf balance the Victorian elements with contemporary chic. In this small space, toiletries are kept to a minimum to avoid clutter.

The look: Inspired by pared-down oriental style, this room achieves its minimalism with modern space-saving fittings, their pipework cleverly concealed behind a false wall underneath the window. A plain and simple colour scheme enhances the clean lines.

Colour: Painting the false wall white allows the suite to blend in with the background and, aided by the natural light that finds its way through the large window, gives the room a bright, airy feel. The aqua-coloured glass partition and the grey, industrial-style floor tiles underline the scheme's modernism by adding smart contemporary colour and texture, while the pale ash panelling softens the look slightly with subtle wood tones.

Suite: An up-to-the-minute suite with smooth curves will give the smallest bathroom a sleek look. Try to fit the bath, basin and loo in a line to give you as much clear floor space as possible. The false wall that encases the loo cistern and the pipework of the semi-recessed basin gives the room an especially streamlined appearance. It also creates a deep multipurpose ledge, which serves as storage and display area, basin countertop and windowsill.

Wood panelling: Tongue-and-groove panelling is commonly found in country-style bathrooms, but these pale ash boards, hung horizontally, give a sleek modern look. Protect them from water by applying several layers of matt polyurethane varnish.

Accessories: With no space for a mirror near the basin, a tall chrome totem topped by a small shaving mirror provides a neat solution. With a shelf for toiletries, plus a rail for clothes or towels, it comprises several accessories in one and is easy to move around. A potted orchid reflects the room's oriental inspiration.

BATHROOM TIP
Planning is the most important aspect of fitting out a bathroom. To optimize your space, take advantage of the expert advice and computer-aided design packages offered by some bathroom companies

The look: A tiny bathroom may present you with limited layout options, but clever design ideas can make it feel less cramped. Simple decor, large mirrors and unobtrusive glass shelving help to maximize the space in this narrow room.

Colour: In a very small room, restrict your main palette to just two plain shades – you can always add tiny amounts of accent colour to liven up the look. White is an obvious choice if you want to increase the feeling of space; this room softens the effect by teaming it with a calming shade of aqua. Using the two shades as plain blocks of colour keeps the look simple – the white is used for the tiles and upper walls, while the green covers all the wood-panelled surfaces.

Suite: The loo slots neatly into the alcove at the end of the room, but the standard-width bath leaves only a very narrow area alongside. A tapered bath may be a better option in a cramped room; while allowing plenty of space at the tap end, where you stand to use the shower attachment, it narrows towards the other to increase floor space.

Shelves: As well as having clean, contemporary appeal, glass shelves give a more open look than those made from solid materials. These are supported by discreet white brackets that blend in with the wall.

Mirror: Every bathroom needs at least one mirror, so make full use of their space-enhancing properties. Large mirrors visually expand a small room by reflecting space and light, and placing one on a long wall in a narrow room like this can make it feel twice as wide.

The look: Every bathroom needs storage, and with clever planning you can fit plenty into even the smallest space. This room uses built-in units to provide cube storage and cupboard space as well as to enclose the concealed parts of the loo, bidet and basin.

Colour: A mix of smart but relaxing neutrals gives the room its sophisticated contemporary character. The dark grey panelling and black countertop create an air of urban chic and highlight the elegant lines of the white suite. The warmer beige of the wall cupboards has a more easy-going feel, while the flecked carpet combines both key colours to add a hint of cosy texture.

Suite: The smooth oval curves of the suite are complemented by chrome taps with stylish conical tops, and the loo completes the look of modern simplicity with a neat push-button flush. A semi-inset basin and back-to-wall loo can be built into fitted units, which ensure clean lines by hiding away the cistern and pipework. Some bathroom companies supply units and bath panels designed to accompany their suites; the ones in this room come primed and ready to paint in your choice of colour.

Storage: Fitting a unit around a basin makes good use of the area below; this one has cupboard doors that allow access to storage space inside. On the wall above, a grid of wooden cubes with flat painted doors provides further unobtrusive storage.

Floor: Although it makes a warm and comfortable floorcovering, carpet may not stand up well to steam and splashes. Avoid deep-pile designs, fit an underlay to ensure good wear and keep a bath mat handy to protect the surface.

The look: Rehanging the door made way for a more user-friendly layout in this small room. Decorating throughout in similar shades enhances the new-found sense of space, while simple modern storage cubes turn clutter into art.

Layout: The door previously opened to the right, which severely restricted the layout options. Rehanging the door allows for a neater layout, with the bath, basin and loo in a line along one wall. Hanging a door so that it opens outwards, rather than into the bathroom, would save even more space.

Colour: Light rosy shades take the chill off a room without having the cramping effect of deeper pinks. To retain a sense of space, stick to a palette of similar shades, rather than heavy contrasts which will appear to cut the room into sections. The dusky wall colour is repeated in the mottled splashback tiles, and tones harmoniously with the neutral stone flooring. Further natural colour and texture is added by the woven window blind and storage boxes.

Suite: Compact fittings with clean lines fit easily into the space available. The loo has a slim, modern cistern, which takes up little horizontal wall space, leaving plenty of room for the basin. A glass shower screen allows an unobstructed view across the room.

Storage: Simple MDF cubes require little wall space but provide useful storage and display areas. To make them, cut pieces of 9mm-thick MDF for each side and sand the edges lightly. Drill small pilot holes in each side and screw the boxes together. Paint with an eggshell finish, then hang from mirror plates.

BATHROOM TIP
Using large-scale furnishings in a small room can trick the eye. Big tiles appear to enlarge a floor area, while hanging a sizeable picture on the wall may also create a surprisingly spacious feel

The look: With a sophisticated shower unit and designer fittings, this room is the height of high-tech. It also shows how effectively white walls and mirrored and glass surfaces can boost the impression of space and light.

Colour: The bright blue flooring, with its wacky wave design, brings colour and a touch of fun to the pristine white environment. The clean, clinical quality of the decor suits the room's high-tech style, but white has also been chosen because it has the ability to make a space feel brighter and airier than any other colour.

Suite: Designed by Philippe Starck, the distinctive modern shapes of the loo and basin add to the room's space-age feel. The more conventional bath is neatly boxed in beside the shower unit with a simple white panel. Mirrored walls create a waterproof splashback which, by reflecting the entire room, makes it feel

considerably more spacious than it actually is.

Shower: The shower unit is another miracle of reflection, with mirrors covering its inside walls and a clear glass door that lets light flow freely. Shower unit doors should be made from toughened safety glass.

Floor: The flooring is Marmoleum, a lino-style covering made from natural raw materials such as linseed oil, chalk and pine resin. It is available in many colours and designs, but this wavy pattern has been created by cutting out dark blue and white shapes and inserting them mosaic-style into the bright blue background.

BATHROOM TIP
If you want a shower that's separate from your bath but can't fit in both, consider placing a freestanding unit elsewhere. A self-contained shower enclosure can slot into an understairs cupboard or a corner of a bedroom, as long as there is adequate ventilation

The look: How do you squeeze standard-sized fittings and plenty of storage into a room of just 1.3 x 2m and still achieve a refreshingly spacious feel? Careful planning, clever shopping and a light-friendly colour scheme can make that dream a reality.

Colour: Fuss-free white walls and matching sanitaryware can work like magic in a small room, creating a bright, contemporary scheme that really opens up the space. However, don't get too hung up on the plain and simple idea – a dash of decoration saves a tiny bathroom from that broom-cupboard feeling. Mosaic-effect wall tiles, with an elegant leafy border, lift the look by adding pattern, texture and interest. The timber countertop also relieves the iciness of the white with its natural warmth.

Suite: Shop around for fittings that suit your needs. This bath tapers slightly at the other end, creating more floor space where it's needed, yet is still big enough for an adult to stretch out in. As the bath falls short of the room's length, a timber box has been created to fill the gap, and this extends to form a countertop for the basin. A semi-recessed basin offers the comfort of a full-sized bowl but can be set into a narrower-than-standard unit to give a feeling of space. Its slick looks are complemented by a modern designer-style mixer tap with easy-to-operate lever control.

Storage: Boxing in the area below the basin creates closed cupboard space for towels and cleaning materials, while the open shelf unit above keeps toiletries more conveniently within reach. Wicker pots add natural character.

The look: With the trend for having more bathrooms within a house, it's tempting to try and squeeze an extra one into a corner of a converted loft. This scheme distracts attention from the room's small proportions by adding character with colour. A skylight window helps to brighten the atmosphere.

Colour: A deep shade of lilac has a stimulating effect in such a small space, and is used on both the walls and ceiling for maximum impact. However, it does not seem too overpowering: applying it as a colourwash helps to soften its strength, and it is balanced with plenty of fresh white. The wide white horizontal stripes break up the expanse of lilac and heighten the vibrant contrast between the two colours. Towels enliven the white suite with accents of hot pink, while metal accessories and wooden details add hints of natural colour and texture.

Suite: Although the wide basin and loo cistern seem rather a tight fit in this small space, the traditional mouldings and generous proportions of the suite have a certain air of luxury about them that adds to the style of the room. There's nothing to stop you placing fittings in close proximity side by side as long as you allow enough sitting or standing space in front for them to serve their purpose.

Window: Loft rooms have a reputation for being dingy, so if you plan to convert yours, it's worth getting skylight windows fitted in the sloping roof. Unless your room is overlooked from above they won't need dressing, although you can buy blinds specially designed for them.

BATHROOM TIP
Before planning a loft conversion, ask your local authority whether you need planning permission. If it's to include a bathroom, seek the advice of an experienced plumber before any work begins

The look: However small your bathroom, don't let size cramp your style. Distinctive furnishings, such as a glass basin and round mosaic tiles, will outshine its tiny dimensions. The boy/girl bath mat and wordy shower curtain add graphic detail to this slick modern scheme.

Colour: Aqua blue is a popular choice for contemporary bathrooms. Cool but welcoming, this mid-tone shade creates a bold impact which is balanced by the lighter colours of the off-white mosaic tiles and pale blue glass-effect laminate flooring.

Suite: The room is just wide enough to fit a standard-sized 170cm bath along one side. A wall-mounted basin frees up floor space; although relatively pricey, this glass bowl in azure blue makes a stylish focal point. A close-coupled loo also saves space. Its sleek shape goes perfectly with the slightly industrial look of the room, as do the wall-mounted spout and crosshead tap controls.

Splashback: Round mosaic tiles are more expensive than standard square ones, but in a tiny space they give priceless individuality. Using coloured grout – these white tiles are finished with grey – also gives an original look.

Storage: A clever chrome over-loo unit utilizes space that is normally wasted. It has rungs for hanging towels, and shelves of varying depths for toiletries, plus a cupboard with frosted glass doors for items best kept hidden. Another practical idea is a freestanding ladder on wheels which can be placed over the radiator to dry towels.

BATHROOM TIP
To form a clean edge when grouting mosaic tiles, place a piece of card or board the same thickness as the tiles along the finished edge. Grout up to and over the card, then carefully remove it

The look: Deep colour can work wonders in small spaces, adding drama, warmth and character. In this oriental-style room, boxing in the suite ensures clean lines, allowing pale wood, buff mosaic and rose pink to create a welcoming mix.

Colour: Although light, cool colours give the illusion of space, deep, warm shades will make your room feel cosier. To enhance the space you have, choose plain shades rather than patterned, and balance a deep colour with pale wood or lighter tiles. Bronze mosaics tone closely with birch panelling to give the lower half of this room a uniform look. Although less intense than the pink, they are rich enough to complement its warmth, bringing a glow to the whole room. Ceramic floor tiles in a pale neutral provide a calmer base.

Suite: Compact fittings with simple modern taps suit this minimalist look, but it's the structures around them that give the room its character. Combining natural warmth with streamlined styling, birch laminate panels fixed onto battens are used to box in both the bath and basin, a door below the basin giving access to useful storage capacity inside. Adding a small partition between the basin and bath helps to break up the space, and could even be fully tiled to form a practical shower screen. Continuing the mosaic tiling onto the tops of the surrounds gives a neat, water-resistant finish.

Accessories: Bamboo accessories reinforce the room's oriental feel. To make bamboo cupboard handles, screw two blocks of plywood to the door, then glue short lengths of bamboo to these using heavy-duty adhesive. Other accessories such as stone pots, woven baskets and a simple flower arrangement are also in character.

BATHROOM TIP
Adding small dividing walls not only adds interest to a room but can also make it easier to plan a space-saving layout. If existing wall area is limited, a partition beside a bath, for instance, can create a surface to sit a basin against

The look: A small space doesn't mean you can't think big. This room manages to fit in a large bath and basin as well as carrying off some bold floor and wall tiles. A calming blend of aqua greens brings them all into harmony.

Colour: The mix of greens and blues creates a refreshing but relaxing atmosphere in this small, dark bathroom. The pale aqua green walls keep the mood airy, while the bath is painted a deeper shade for contrast. Dark blue floor tiles smarten up the look, and the medley of watery green wall tiles also packs a punch.

Suite: If you want to fit a large bath into a small space, opt for depth over length. A roll-top bath combines character with a generous bathing area, and can be painted to match your scheme. Don't let size dictate the agenda when it comes to other fittings; a tiny modern basin may save space, but this sturdy traditional design makes a much better partner for the period-style bath.

Splashback: Less is often more when it comes to wall tiles. In a cramped space, a large expanse of colourful tiling might look overpowering, whereas a small splashback above a basin adds just enough impact. Using fewer tiles also means you can afford to indulge in pricey but beautiful handmade designs.

Floor: The same principle applies to flooring: with only a small area to cover, you might find the pennies to splash out on a style-statement floorcovering. Real stone tiles are expensive to buy, and should be professionally fitted, but these silvery blue slate slabs fit in perfectly with the colour scheme.

The look: Clever use of colour and a suite designed for small spaces help to broaden the horizons of this narrow bathroom, which measures just 1.2m wide. Boxed-in pipework and a neat storage cabinet also contribute to its clean, contemporary look.

Colour: Three shades of green give the room a bright but soothing atmosphere, and form a subtle contrast with the white suite and mosaic tiles. Painting the shades in broad bands around the walls makes the room feel wider, a useful decorating trick if you want to expand a narrow space.

Suite: Tiny bathrooms are a common breed, so manufacturers are responding to the demand for scaled-down fittings. This tiny suite includes a bath only 119cm long, just the right size to fit across the width of the room. The loo and basin, also smaller than most other models, have been fitted side by side to allow a clear run of floor space through from the door to the bath.

Wood panelling: Exposed pipework looks bad enough in a large bathroom, but in an area of this size it's a real eyesore. Boxing in the pipes with tongue-and-groove boards not only keeps them out of sight but also creates an extra shelf. The bath is boxed in too, and painting all the panelling to match the adjacent band of wall colour gives the lower part of the room a clean, seamless appearance.

Storage: Make efficient use of space with multifunctional items, such as cabinet doors that double as mirrors. This wall-mounted cupboard swallows up toiletries and cosmetics, leaving basin and bath surrounds clear and preventing clutter from killing the sensation of space.

The look: Country-style accessories and dashes of ginger add spice to this cream bathroom. The towel rail and minimal window dressing also warm things up by boosting heat and light levels.

Colour: Decorating with cream not only makes a small space feel bright and airy but also creates a go-with-anything backdrop. If you like to change your decor frequently, it's simpler to renew accessories rather than repaint walls or tiles. Window dressings, towels and soaps all offer easy ways of introducing character-forming colour. Here a Roman blind in crisp ginger and white ticking adds spicy warmth to the window area, while a burnt orange bath towel makes a bolder statement. Other accessories enhance the country feel with natural colour.

Bath: Boxing in a bath with wood panelling gives a neat look and allows you to paint the surround to match your walls. If you have the space, including a ledge around the top of the bath creates an attractive display area for pretty accessories.

Towel rail: The heated towel rail beside the bath means that warm, dry towels are never far away. If you want a rail that will heat your room as well, choose a model designed to double as a radiator. Towel rails come in many sizes – a tall one provides ample hanging space.

Accessories: A country look relies on natural materials and textures as well as colours. A bamboo bath rack makes a perfect finishing touch, and the woven laundry basket and stone candleholder also reinforce the look.

The look: Look to foreign lands for colourful country style. This bathroom's maritime scheme was inspired by the vibrant blues and greens of the seas around Greece. Panelled walls and painted wooden furniture show them off beautifully.

Colour: Different tones of blue mix comfortably together, and greens blend well with them to create a harmonious scheme. A spectrum of sea shades gives this room its welcoming, summery feel – from deepest indigo on the bath to brighter blue and jade on wood panelling and furniture, through to soft aqua on the upper walls. Using a lighter shade for the top half of the room helps to freshen the atmosphere.

Wall panelling: Wood panelling creates a warmer, more natural feel than tiled walls, and is widely used in country-style rooms. As tongue-and-groove boards can be painted in any colour, they make a versatile wallcovering that can be decorated to suit a variety of different moods. This dado-height panelling is edged with a wide wooden beading that provides a useful display area for seashore accessories such as shells and starfish.

Suite: A traditional roll-top bath is ideal for creating that old-fashioned, unfitted feel and, like the wall panelling, can be painted to boost the room's colour power. A wood-effect seat adds rustic style to the loo.

Furniture: Keep the colour show going by painting old wooden furniture. Sand down the wood, or use a multi-surface primer if it's already painted or varnished, then apply gloss or satin-finish colour. Add a coat of varnish as protection against splashes of water. The simple green chest has been further revamped by adding a wavy plinth cut from MDF, plus new wooden drawer knobs.

The look: A complete white-wash will open up a small bathroom, making it feel amazingly bright and spacious. To prevent it feeling cold, subtle colour accents and characterful accessories have been added.

Colour: Painting both walls and ceiling in white will certainly appear to expand space. If this idea appeals, add interest with textured surfaces – wood panelling looks less clinical than white tiles, and the woven chair has natural texture. Colour accents lift the look, but this scheme retains its understated calm by sticking to neutral shades. The greys of the patterned flooring are echoed by the silvery glimmer of the taps and metallic items. Wooden accessories add warmer splashes of colour.

Suite: The traditional design of the suite and taps also helps to soften the look, creating a more laid-back feel than sleek modern fittings. Boxing in the bath with panelling that matches the walls creates a streamlined effect.

Chair: The classic Lloyd Loom chair adds an air of old-fashioned comfort. If you want to change the colour of a woven chair, use spray paint. Work in a well-ventilated room and cover surrounding surfaces, then apply several light coats.

Accessories: Choose accessories that add character as well as colour. For a lived-in feel, include items that have seen better days, such as the old mirror and distressed medicine cabinet. The folding stool adds a further casual touch, in contrast with the smarter metal accessories.

The look: Wooden floorboards and wall panelling painted in cool cream give this bathroom an airy modern-country feel, while louvred shutters and carved wood add touches of colonial style.

Colour: Light colours create a sense of space, and cream gives a clean and simple look that's easy to live with. The wood-panelled walls and bath surround are painted with eggshell to match the sanded floorboards, giving the small room a spacious, streamlined feel. A closely toning shade on the walls continues the seamless look, while a sparkling white suite crisps up the cream. Accents of rich terracotta and dark brown add hints of exotic style to warm up the cool surroundings.

Suite: The suite teams classic Victorian styling with lean contours, which save space in a relatively small room. Panelling the bath with tongue-and-groove boards and opting for a mahogany-effect loo seat gives the fittings a softer, country-style appearance.

Furniture: A dark wood Moroccan cupboard and a pine-framed mirror, both with decorative carving, add character to the room. The wall-mounted cabinet with glass-panelled doors provides tidy storage for toiletries while keeping its contents on view. It is painted to match the scheme, with cream on the outside and terracotta inside.

Window: Colonial-style shutters complement the ethnic appeal of the Moroccan cupboard. Their adjustable louvred panels allow full control over light levels.

The look: Make that holiday mood last all year round with a bathroom that brings the seaside closer to home. A candy-striped deck chair and a sky-blue tub, cast adrift on a sea of ocean-blue flooring, are constant reminders of lazy days on the beach.

Colour: Floorboards painted in deep blue and finished with clear varnish have the colour and shimmering quality of calm seas, and unfitted furniture shows them off to advantage. They are complemented by the paler blue used to highlight the bath, while the soft lilac on the lower walls enhances the relaxing feel of the scheme. White provides a crisp contrast, bringing a breath of fresh air to the room, and the pretty pink stripes of the deck chair also help to lighten the mood.

Bath: A large, old-fashioned bath is the central feature of this laid-back look. What's more, its shape is reminiscent of the hull of a boat. The burnished gold finish on its feet introduces a luxurious touch of glamour.

Chair: Who says deck chairs are only for outdoors? Imaginative use of furniture is an easy way of adding character to a bathroom, and this chair gives an instant seaside feel. If you want to replace the sling of a deck chair to match your scheme, choose a tough canvas or other strong cotton fabric.

Accessories: The large wall map above the bath hints romantically at distant shores, while its aqua background introduces a further dose of sea-inspired colour.

BATHROOM TIP
Cast-iron baths are not only extremely durable but also retain heat better than acrylic fittings, which means your bath water stays hotter for longer

The look: Pretty florals and delicate pastels set the tone for a comfortable country-cottage bathroom steeped in tradition. Slip in modern materials such as Perspex and laminate to edge the look into the 21st century.

Colour: Pastels such as muted pinks, mint green and lilacs form the colour palette for this feminine look, but its most important ingredient is flowers. Look for traditional floral patterns, especially on wallpaper. If you want to combine a number of different prints, give your scheme a unified look by making sure they all contain one common colour, such as pink. To prevent the scheme becoming over-fussy, offset the floral walls and fabric with plenty of plain colour in painted or tiled surfaces.

Suite: No hard lines are allowed for this look, so choose a suite with curvy contours. A rounded modern basin looks perfectly at home in this nostalgic setting when teamed with traditional taps in gleaming chrome. The semi-countertop design is built into a wooden unit painted in pale green to match the chair and bath surround. Wood-effect laminate gives the top a waterproof covering, while a Perspex splashback protects the wallpaper.

Floor: Ceramic tiles provide hard-wearing, low-maintenance flooring and give a clean, contemporary look. To complement the pastel palette, choose a soft, livable neutral that looks relaxingly natural rather than rustic.

Accessories: Shower caps and washbags offer the opportunity to introduce further floral romance, while wicker baskets and touches of wood give country authenticity. Add comfort with a painted wooden chair with rush seat, plus fluffy towels in natural or pretty colours. Scented toiletries with old-fashioned packaging complete the look.

BATHROOM TIP
Displaying well-chosen toiletries is an easy way of adding character or colour to your room. Many brands have smart or decorative packaging, while bath oils come in a range of delicious colours, from modern brights to country-style neutrals

The look: Inspired by chic 1930s looks, this simple but sophisticated scheme combines a smart Art Deco-style suite with a more decorative Arts and Crafts feel created by wood-panelled walls and floral details.

Colour: Light blue makes a refreshing choice for this small bathroom, filling it with uplifting colour without compromising its feeling of space. Pale grey flooring harmonizes with the cool blue to give the overall look a calming effect, while the white suite provides a crisp contrast.

Walls: Panelling the walls up to picture-rail height makes the small but high-ceilinged room look more in proportion by breaking up the vertical space. This effect has been emphasized by painting the wall above the panelling a few tones lighter and topping it with a plate rack detail that provides a display space for decorative accessories. The panelling comprises waterproof MDF boards made to look like tongue and groove.

Suite: A loo with angular lines inspired by Art Deco design adds shape and style. The chunky bath also makes its presence felt, its outsize dimensions defying the limited space within the room to instil an air of luxury. Panelling it to match the walls makes it look less imposing by helping it to blend in with the background.

Accessories: The row of pretty floral pictures on the plate rack creates an eye-catching display and picks up on the Arts and Crafts influence. They are made from swatches of fabric slipped into white-painted wooden frames. A floral-print laundry bag echoes their country charm, while other accessories, such as the chrome laundry bin and glass-fronted medicine cabinet, have a sleeker, contemporary feel.

The look: The earthy colours and textures of old Provençal buildings inspired this casual country look, where a curvy modern suite blends comfortably with distressed furniture and rustic, stone-like effects on walls and floor.

Colour: Gentle colours of nature – sage green, warm terracotta and pale neutrals – give the room its relaxing atmosphere. However, it's the textural effects that create the timeworn charm of a traditional French farm-house. Softly colourwashed walls have the look of old sandstone, while the ceramic floor tiles are designed to resemble real terracotta. Painting the vanity unit and shutters with a distressed finish gives a deliberately shabby look.

Paint effects: For a colourwash like this, select two shades of sand-coloured emulsion, one light, the other several shades darker. Apply the paler colour and leave to dry. Dilute the other with water until it is the strength you want, then apply using a wide brush and crisscross strokes. To distress wooden furniture, paint with a pale neutral shade, then rub candlewax on areas that might suffer wear, such as panel edges. Apply green paint, then rub back the waxed parts with wire wool to expose patches of base coat.

Suite: Sleek contemporary fittings and taps add an air of modern comfort to this traditional setting, their rounded curves enhancing the room's relaxed feel. Building the basin into a distressed vanity unit heightens the contrast between old and new.

Accessories: Glazed terracotta pots, slipware bowls and chunky natural-coloured soaps help to create the Provençal feel. More unusual details, such as the candelabra, add character. If they're in season, fresh sunflowers arranged in a toning pitcher add the perfect finishing touch.

The look: Glowing yellow and other primary hues brighten up this tiny bathroom with the feelgood shades and vivid colour contrasts of the Caribbean. Lightly whitewashed tongue-and-groove panelling re-creates the sun-bleached look of a tropical beach-house.

Colour: The brilliant yellow on the walls ensures that the sun never stops shining, a guaranteed cure for a dingy bathroom. In a small room, balancing this strong shade with plenty of fresh white helps to maintain the feeling of space. The large picture that covers most of one wall softens the strength of the yellow but livens up the look with additional vibrant colour, its big abstract blocks lending the room a strikingly modern feel. Dark blue bath towels also add impact by creating a strong contrast with the yellow.

Wood panelling: The tongue-and-groove panelling on the side of the bath and the lower part of the walls offsets the powerful colours and abstract art to give the room a more relaxed, rural atmosphere. The white paint finish preserves the natural appeal of the wood by allowing the grain and knotting to show through, suggesting a sun-bleached appearance. To get this effect, simply dilute white emulsion with water – add a little at a time and experiment on scrap boarding until you achieve the strength you want. When the painted panelling is dry, protect it from damp by applying a few coats of clear matt varnish.

Accessories: A crude storage box, made from an old wooden packing crate mounted on the wall, enhances the room's driftwood appeal, while the big seashell on top directly links its inspiration to tropical shores.

The look: If traditional country style is too fussy for your taste but you want a bathroom with plenty of interest, try this relaxing look that combines pale, modern colours and a contemporary suite with natural textures and accessories.

Colour: The refreshing aqua on the walls is offset by the soft, natural colour of the splashback tiles, creating a light but inviting atmosphere. Paler colour schemes in bathrooms can tend to look rather stark and cold, especially with white woodwork, but this is counteracted by textural touches, such as the green slate-effect flooring and linen blind. Dark wood isn't always the first choice for bathroom accessories but the mahogany-coloured cabinet helps to add definition to the overall look.

Suite: With a versatile contemporary design that would suit a range of different settings, the fittings combine clean styling with gentle curves, and the modern taps have simple rounded controls in white. The hand-held shower attachment can be fixed into a holder just above the bath when it's not in use.

Window: If your room has only a small window, you can afford to dress it with a gorgeous fabric, especially if making it into a Roman blind, which requires a minimal amount of material. The good-quality linen used to make this blind adds texture and pattern to the scheme but is fine enough to let plenty of light filter through.

Accessories: The dark wood cabinet cuts down on clutter by providing a home for toiletry supplies, and its barred, see-through doors help to keep them in sight and mind. Sisal and seagrass baskets supplement the natural textures in the room as well as providing storage for laundry and smaller items.

The look: You don't have to scatter shells everywhere to bring a breath of sea air into your bathroom. Blue and white, the colours of ocean, sky and surf, are all you need to create a marine feel, a theme hinted at in this room by the seagull print above the bath.

Colour: Although blue is a cool colour, deeper shades can create an inviting atmosphere. The blue on the wood panelling sets the tone for a warm, summery feel, while lighter shades on the upper walls and floor keep the overall effect bright and airy. The white suite stands out beautifully against the deep background, and crisply contrasts with the rich wood colours of the loo seat and cabinet, which add a strong air of tradition to the scheme.

Wood panelling: The tongue-and-groove panelling on the lower walls has been fitted over old tiles, avoiding the tedious job of removing them. If you want to attempt a similar cover-up, add wide wooden beading along the top of the panels to conceal the tile edges and give a neat finish.

Suite: The suite enhances the room's comforting traditional atmosphere – its classic style is denoted by angular lines and curved mouldings, a mahogany-effect loo seat and old-fashioned pillar tap controls. The bath is panelled with tongue-and-groove painted in the same shade as the upper walls.

Accessories: Metallic accessories echo the gleaming chrome taps: the toothbrush tumbler and loo-roll holder add sparkle and shine, while a curly wire magazine rack provides a home for reading matter beside the loo. The dark wood storage cabinet and decorative wall lamps add to the traditional elements in the room.

The look: Imagine you're bathing in a country stream as you lie back and watch fish leaping around you or feast your eyes on the natural greens and browns of leaves and bark. Country house elegance takes on the great outdoors in this original scheme.

Colour: A blend of greens, greys and wood tones re-creates that woodland feel. The emphasis is on natural materials, including the dark grey marble flooring, wood-effect bath panelling and natural-fibre rug. The deep pine greens of the chair and lower wall decoration tone with the flooring. On the upper part of the walls, pale green sets a more refreshing mood, teaming up with the white ceiling and splashback to keep the overall look light and airy. A richly patterned blind adds definition to the window and echoes accents of russet and yellow introduced in accessories.

Walls: Stencils and paint effects add plenty of interest to the walls. The lower section is decorated with a jade green marbled effect that echoes the flooring. Applied in blocks, it mimics the panelled walls of an old country house. Above this, a lively border of stencilled fish motifs runs around the room, while a more subtle design outlines the top of the walls. Whatever your room theme, specialist stencil companies are almost certain to stock a motif that suits it, and can also supply the paints and brushes to apply it.

Accessories: The theme of fishy goings-on continues with the quirky shelf brackets, which reflect the shape of the stencil motif. Pile on rustic texture in mats, pots, sponges and loofahs. For extra outdoor authenticity, add items that come straight from the natural world, such as plants and pieces of driftwood.

The look: Boat designs on pictures and fabrics, along with a bright and breezy colour scheme, give this bathroom its jaunty nautical air – just what you need to set your sails flapping first thing in the morning.

Colour: Deep turquoise and dazzling white make an invigorating combination. Balancing them equally allows the clean white splashback tiles and suite to counteract the richness of the turquoise walls and bath panel, giving the overall look a refreshing feel. The dark blue background of the window blind also forms a vibrant contrast with the turquoise and makes an effective foil for its jazzy boat motifs in primary colours. Its border echoes the sandy tones of the carpet.

Suite: A close-coupled loo, with no connecting pipe separating the cistern and bowl, has a neat appearance. Boxing in the pipework alongside and continuing the

white tiling over its housing also gives the room a shipshape look. Unfussy wooden bath panelling, painted to match the walls, adds to the room's casual country character.

Window: Although soft furnishing features in a bathroom are relatively limited, window dressings can play a key role in enhancing its theme or colour scheme. A bold print works well at a wide window, and a simple Roman blind shows it off to advantage. Textured window panes guarantee privacy even when the blind is raised.

Accessories: Colourful boat and harbour pictures echo the blind design, and wide white frames lend them emphasis against the turquoise walls. The long windowsill offers plenty of space for a display of natural accessories: plants in terracotta pots conceal the central window frames, while pots of pebbles and shells underline the seaside theme.

The look: Box in a simple white suite with wood panelling, and you're halfway to creating a look that's pure country. Rustic wooden accessories, simple toiletries and jugs of fresh flowers complete the picture.

Colour: Mellow yellow is the perfect choice for a cheerful country scheme – as well as evoking a sunny corn-meadow feel, it blends beautifully with natural wood tones. Using the same shade on all the woodwork creates a plain and simple backdrop for the numerous small accessories that contribute character to this look. The floorboards and the upper part of the walls balance the warmth of the yellow with a cool off-white, helping to maintain a feeling of space and height.

Suite: If modern sanitaryware looks too functional for your taste, try a hide-and-disguise job with painted wood. Tongue-and-groove boards create a cosy, country-cabin look and make a low-cost, easy-to-fit covering for baths as well as walls. If you're a skilled woodworker, you could probably also build your own vanity unit around a basin. If not, try to find a local carpenter who can make one to your design. This traditional-style cupboard was created using MDF, plus ready-made panelled doors, which give access to storage space beneath the basin.

Accessories: Have fun with accessories if you like a homely look. Decorative items, such as the bird and ship ornaments, add individuality, while the framed postcards introduce a touch of nostalgia. Reinforce the rustic feel with driftwood frames, earthenware containers and simply packaged toiletries in natural colours. Shaker furnishings are great for any country scheme – the wooden rocking chair combines comfort with style, while a peg rail provides hanging space.

BATHROOM TIP
Pictures and ornaments give traditional-style bathrooms an inviting feel but make sure any treasured items will tolerate a steamy atmosphere. You can protect paintings or photos by framing them behind glass or Perspex

The look: A selection of brilliant pinks and yellows and a lively wallpaper patterned with bathroom bits and pieces create a bright, wide-awake look. Retro patterns and colours give the room a fun 1950s flavour but the streamlined wall-mounted suite brings it bang up to date.

Colour: A wallpaper or fabric design can form a good starting point for a room scheme. If you choose to cover your walls with a busy or distinctive pattern, keep the rest of the decor simple – balancing it with a bold, plain colour picked out from the design will create a striking impact. Hot pink forms a vibrant contrast for the white suite and floor tiles, and fitting the wooden boarding horizontally adds to the room's individual style.

Suite: Wall-mounted fittings give a particularly neat look,

especially if they have clean, contemporary curves and compact proportions. The loo cistern and other workings are hidden behind the wood panelling, and a half pedestal encloses pipework below the basin. The flush is operated by a discreet push-button control fixed into the ledge above the panelling. Choosing a wall-mounted suite means the loo and bidet can be fixed at a height to suit you, and also makes it easier to clean the floor beneath. Taps with tall spouts are convenient for smaller fittings as they stand clear of the basin area.

Accessories: Many furnishing ranges offer accessories such as bathrobes and washbags to match their wallcoverings or fabrics. Team these with plain towels, beakers and vases that contribute dashes of further colour picked out from the wallpaper design.

BATHROOM TIP
Make sure that panelling fitted around sanitaryware can be easily removed to allow instant access to any boxed-in plumbing if it should need repairs

The look: White-painted wooden boarding, trelliswork door panels and leafy potted palms give this bathroom the airy elegance of a Victorian summerhouse. A big sink and marble countertops make it a place to luxuriate in.

Colour: Wall-to-wall white creates a beautifully fresh feel, although it can look monotonous and clinical. This room counteracts that adverse effect by punctuating the white surfaces with textural pattern – the lines of the wood panelling on the walls and the trelliswork designs of the door fronts. These add plenty of interest so that additional colour can be kept to a minimum. Only the subtle greys of the marble countertops and flooring, plus a few accents in plants and accessories, interrupt the expanse of pure white.

Suite: A rectangular basin with generous proportions has an air of traditional luxury that complements the styling of the room. The pillar taps also have classic-style controls. By contrast, the loo's compact modern design makes it look neat and unobtrusive, especially with the cistern concealed inside a wooden housing.

Fitted units: With cupboards fitted below and beside the basin, and on the wall, this bathroom enjoys plenty of storage space. The panelled and trelliswork doors exude classic elegance, but a similar look could be created quite cheaply. Use MDF to build the carcasses, then look for ready-made panelled doors – some kitchen companies sell these on their own, without units. Replace some of the inner panels with MDF trelliswork, available from DIY stores, then paint everything white before fitting the doors. More trelliswork has been used to make shutters for the windows and a cover for the radiator below the sill.

BATHROOM TIP
If you buy sanitaryware from different sources, make sure the pieces you choose are all a similar shade. Even whites can vary in tone, especially among older fittings

The look: A suite with unusual octagonal shaping is offset by equally distinctive decor in a room that brings a designer touch to rustic style. The natural grain and texture of wood plays a starring role, with the walls and window dressed with panels that look as if they've been hewn straight from the log.

Colour: The glowing tones of the dramatic wood panelling give the room a warm and welcoming atmosphere, while the chocolate browns of the low wall and ceramic floor tiles lend the look a sophisticated feel. An absence of further colour reinforces the impact of the woody browns and the smart simplicity of the scheme, although the black and white cow-print bag adds a quirky touch of modernity.

Suite: The suite brings traditional style into the 21st century. The fittings feature an octagonal outline with distinct lines and very flat, even surfaces, which work well in this modern environment. The sleek white fittings are thrown into relief against the dark backdrop, which helps to show off their attractive shape.

Wooden furnishings: The wood panels used in this room were specially produced, but you could create a similar warm and natural effect by covering walls with planks of wood cut to different widths. You could also try dressing a window using sheets of wood veneer. Used for marquetry, and on furniture, they are so thin that light shines through them. Insert an eyelet in the centre of each strip and hang from metal hooks at the top of the window. Complete the look with wooden furniture – whether modern or rustic, anything with beautiful grain will fit the bill.

The look: Wood, wicker and traditional furnishings create an inviting country look. An all-neutral scheme complements the room's rustic character but brings an air of restrained elegance to cottage style – there are no clichéd chintzy florals here.

Colour: Walls with a pale neutral colourwash and oak floorboards with a grey wax finish create a smart but relaxing foil for the warmer tones of the wicker baskets and honey-coloured bath panels. With walls covered in a stylishly patterned woodland-inspired paper, the adjoining loo forms a cosy enclave off the main bathroom. Country-style checks make a subtle appearance as white and taupe splashback tiles around the bath.

Walls: The combination of wallpaper and paint adds interest to the scheme, while choosing similar tones for both gives the adjoining rooms a unified look. If you want a busily patterned paper in a small room but fear that it might overwhelm the space, look for a design with just two colours. The bathroom walls are painted using shades that match the wallpaper – a mixture of artist's acrylics in raw umber, grey and yellow ochre applied as a colourwash using scumble glaze.

Suite: The suite combines clean lines with the substance and shape of a traditional design. The pine-effect finish of the loo seat and the classic-style bath panelling makes it perfect for a country cottage look. The distinctive curves of the basin rim are complemented by an arched splashback moulding, echoed by the rim of the toilet cistern.

Accessories: Wicker baskets and handpainted Spanish jugs enhance the country look, while framed prints add manor-house chic. A wooden table with a distressed paint finish combines storage capacity with character.

BATHROOM TIP
Adding scumble glaze to a colourwash helps to stop diluted paint becoming too weak and runny. It increases the paint's working time, making it easier to achieve the effect you want. Buy it at craft shops or specialist paint stores

The look: Sunlight filtering through white-painted shutters highlights the small gold squares of the wallpaper and the sleek curves of the suite in this scheme that combines elements of colonial style with contemporary glamour.

Colour: A neutral palette bridges the gap between contemporary and colonial as it is a popular choice for both decorating styles. The calming mid-tone background of the wallpaper tones harmoniously with the wooden flooring while providing a warm foil for the white suite and shutters. Its reflective gold squares have a fashionable luminous sheen but also suggest a latticework effect reminiscent of ethnic-style screens. The darker shades of natural accessories add depth to the look.

Suite: The sculptural curves of the suite and the streamlined single-lever taps establish the mood of contemporary chic. The wall-mounted basin is particularly neat, all pipework concealed within its half-pedestal. Discreet Perspex splashbacks protect the wallpaper while letting its design show through. The clear panels are fixed in place with chrome-capped mirror screws.

Floor: Combining trendy looks with tropical overtones, the deck flooring is a clever and effective way of covering a concrete sub-floor. Made from natural teak, it is warm to the touch and develops a beautiful patina as it ages. Simple mats in natural colours help to make it more homely.

Accessories: The louvred shutters and smaller furnishings introduce the truly colonial elements of the look. When the shutters are open, bamboo plants on the balcony offer a screen of privacy with an oriental look. The rattan trunk, basket platter and dark wood mirror frame offset the clean white suite with natural colour and texture, plus decorative country-style design.

BATHROOM TIP
If you like a patterned look but can't face hanging wallpaper, use a rubber stamp to print motifs on plain painted walls. It's quick and easy to do, and DIY and craft stores offer a wide range of stamp designs

The look: A suite with traditional English styling brings an air of subtle elegance to a scheme inspired by Shaker design. Cool cream, warm wood and unfussy furnishings re-create the air of natural simplicity favoured by early New England settlers.

Colour: Cream forms part of the classic Shaker palette, and using it to cover the walls from floor to ceiling creates the calming atmosphere that their design philosophy demands. The white suite and splashback tiles provide a crisp contrast, while the wooden flooring and accessories inject natural warmth to give the pale scheme a welcoming feel.

Suite: The simple decor makes a plain foil for the more elaborate shaping of the suite. Its Edwardian design is based around angular edges and soft curves, with the basin splashback and cistern rim featuring gently sweeping lines. The pedestals have the corners sliced off and are finished with stepped bases. Traditional chrome-plated taps continue the elegant look, but a plain glass panel makes an unobtrusive shower screen.

Floor: The natural grain and colour of wooden flooring make it a popular choice for country-style settings. If you live in an older house, you may be lucky enough to find original floorboards hidden beneath carpet or lino. If they are in good condition, strip them back using sanding machines borrowed from a hire shop. (They come with instructions on how to use them.) Seal the sanded surface with floor varnish to prevent water from penetrating the wood.

Accessories: Fuss-free design, functionality and natural texture are key ingredients for Shaker accessories. A peg rail typifies the style and offers hanging space above the basin. The rustic basket below keeps spare towels handy.

The look: The combination of a traditional white suite, wood panelling and soft sage green walls gives this bathroom a period look that is understated but strong on style. The chequerboard floor design adds a distinctive touch.

Colour: Pine panelling gives a country twist to this classic look. Its natural appeal is complemented by the restful sage green wall colour and the light but warm neutral shade of the splashback tiles. With the room dominated by wood, the floor needed something to give it a lift. Painting it in a solid colour would have unbalanced the look, but this chequerboard pattern adds plenty of character while preserving the beauty of its grain.

Panelling and suite: Classic-style wood panelling makes it easy to create a formal look in a characterless room, and is simple to fix onto walls or around a bath. The semi-recessed basin is built into a matching vanity unit made by a local carpenter, while a wood-effect seat ties the loo into the scheme. Finish wooden surfaces with clear matt varnish to protect them from damp.

Floor: The chequerboard design has transformed an ordinary wooden floor into a stunning feature. To apply the design to sanded boards, first measure and mark out large blocks. Mask off alternate squares and paint these with woodstain in a walnut shade. When dry, remove the masking tape and apply clear floor varnish over the entire surface.

Accessories: Sheer cotton voile curtains give a more dressy look than blinds, and conceal an ugly window without blocking light. Other striking accessories include the mirror with Venetian glass frame and the brass wall sconces, which together create a grand focal point.

The look: Freshen up a small bathroom with a serving of spring greens. In this tiny space measuring just 2 x 2.5m, a cool colour scheme and some imaginative timberwork clear the way for streamlined contemporary style.

Colour: Two shades of apple green give this room its up-to-the-minute appeal. In a restricted space, a simple scheme works best, with the room neatly divided into two blocks of colour. Using the lighter shade above maintains an airy feel, and the white suite also keeps the mood fresh. The wooden grille covering the radiator allows the deeper green used on the wall panelling to continue all around the room. The checked blind adds a contrasting dash of dark blue, highlighting the crispness of the greens.

Suite: Fitting a standard-sized bath left little room for a loo, but a slimline model slots neatly into the space available. With a design inspired by Art Deco style, it teams a curvaceous bowl with a chunky, angular pedestal.

Radiator cover: The radiator is concealed behind a timber screen, painted to match the wall panelling. Its grille lets heat through, and a rail fixed to the front allows the radiator to double as a towel warmer. The ledge along the top provides attractive display space. This cover was custom built, but off-the-peg MDF designs with fretwork fronts can be bought in flatpack form ready to paint.

Window: A double set of blinds makes for a versatile window dressing. The Roman blind can be lowered for complete privacy, whereas the Venetian blind allows finer control over light levels. The checked fabric plays an important role in adding colour and pattern to the scheme.

BATHROOM TIP
No space for a radiator? Consider underfloor heating instead, especially if you are lucky enough to be starting from scratch

COUNTRY

The look: You can almost hear the waves crashing on the shore in this refreshing beachhouse-style bathroom. Painted wooden boarding forms the basis of this simple look.

Colour: A light shade of aqua is perfect for creating a cool, sea-fresh environment. Teamed with white-painted flooring, it makes the room feel as invigorating as a splash in the waves. A cream-coloured suite complements the natural feel, while rustic accessories in dark wood and wicker add texture and depth.

Walls and floor: Tongue-and-groove planks pinned horizontally to the walls give the room a real beachhouse look. For a nautical appearance, paint the wood with several coats of thinned-down emulsion. The floor is painted with diluted white emulsion, which allows the grain of the boards to show through, giving a sun-bleached effect. Protect all wood

surfaces in a bathroom with a coat of varnish.

Suite: With contemporary shaping enhanced by subtle detail, the suite would look at home in many different settings. While its clean curves offer simplicity, the stepped mouldings around the edge of the basin and cistern lid add a more decorative touch. Modern chromium-plated taps enhance its sleek style.

Accessories: Complete the look with natural objects – a mirror framed in driftwood, a weather-beaten stool and an assortment of shells and pebbles will all help to reinforce the seashore theme. Make a fitting display space by edging a shelf with a wavy MDF trim, painted in blue.

The look: A combination of robust blue and minty green creates a bold but refreshing colour scheme for this modern bathroom. Boxing in the fittings helps to give the small, narrow space a streamlined look, enhancing the air of contemporary cool.

Colour: The bright blue tiles that run from the window to the basin form a vibrant block of colour in contrast with the white fittings. The blue mood continues with a sparkly vinyl floorcovering, but painting the walls in a pale blue as well might have made the room feel too cold. Instead, a fresh minty green lifts the scheme.

Suite: Compact modern fittings economize on space. The back-to-wall loo has its tiny cistern hidden inside a framework, which forms a handy shelf for bath oils. To create further storage, the semi-recessed basin is surrounded by a vanity unit with tiled countertop. This unit,

the bath surround and the loo housing were all built to order by a local carpenter.

Window: As the only source of natural light, the small window needs a dressing that will keep the room bright by day but provide privacy when required. A Venetian blind fits the bill, and this wooden design is stained a pale bluey-green, a perfect match for the walls.

Accessories: Smart chrome accessories, such as the loo-brush holder and bath rack, set the seal on an up-to-the-minute scheme. The mirror above the basin incoporates a sleek shelf for toothpaste and brushes.

BATHROOM TIP
Not enough cash to splash on a suite? Update your old one by fitting slick modern taps, and invest in a matching set of well-designed chrome accessories to get your bathroom sparkling like a new pin

The look: Earthy autumnal shades bring a cosy glow to this high-ceilinged room. The simple storage unit and window blinds set a contemporary mood, and clever disguises make the existing suite blend in by hiding or replacing fussy design details.

Colour: Tall rooms in old houses can feel chilly and uninviting, but a dose of warm colour soon raises the temperature. To make a feature of the picture rail, the untiled wall is painted in three glowing colours: the main part in deep red, the rail a slightly darker shade and the space above in a pale ochre. These rich colours tone beautifully with the knotty pine flooring and skirting board. With plenty of warmth to balance it, the white-tiled wall has a freshening rather than chilling effect, and the earthy browns of the large painting soften it further.

Suite: Dated scallop detailing made the suite a real turn-off, so the curved bath panels have been replaced with painted tongue-and-groove boarding and the shell-shaped loo seat swapped for a simple wooden one. A towelling cushion filled with washable stuffing conceals a scalloped ledge on the bath. Fixed in place with two suction caps, it acts as a headrest.

Storage: The small compartments of this CD rack are ideal for toiletries, and its adjustable shelving can accommodate items of varying sizes. Tall and slim, it requires little wall space, fitting neatly into the narrow area between two windows.

Windows: Plain white roller blinds score high on contemporary simplicity, and are cheap to buy. They also let plenty of natural light filter through, especially if made from fine cotton.

The look: If you're stuck with a suite in a colour you hate but can't afford to change it, the answer is to decorate the rest of the room in shades that make it easier to live with.

Colour: The outdated dark green suite in this bathroom had to stay, but a complete whitewash has freshened up the gloomy decor that surrounded it. White not only makes a small bathroom feel light and bright, but also goes with any other colour, and creates a clean foil for dark or dull-coloured fittings. This simple scheme plays up the contrast between the walls and suite with the addition of green accents in accessories.

Tiles: Why go to the trouble of removing old wall tiles? If all you want to do is change the colour of plain, flat tiles, the easiest way is to paint them. Clean them thoroughly with sugar soap and allow to dry, then apply tile primer followed by a top coat of tile or gloss paint – applying it with a small roller will give an even finish. If you want to fit textured or patterned tiles, you can lay them over the old ones, using a wooden strip or pieces of tile to conceal the double thickness. Ensure that the original tiles are stuck firmly before you start.

Accessories: A set of simple wooden shelves, painted to blend in with the walls, allows for a display of accessories that add both colour and character. Metallic items, such as the chrome Venetian blind, vases and candle sconces, not only complement the cool greens but also reflect light, making the tiny room feel even brighter.

BATHROOM TIP
Although popular in the 1970s, coloured suites are a definite no-no nowadays, so it's worth replacing them if you can afford to. Crisp white fittings will go with any decor, outlast fashion fads and could be a selling point if you put your home on the market

The look: A flash of budget-wise brilliance brings a small bathroom bang up to date. Red and purple introduce zingy colour without overpowering the tiny space, while a few simple and inexpensive improvements give the existing suite a new lease of life.

Colour: Basing a scheme on white increases the sense of space, but adding moderate amounts of vivid colour will transform the look. A red and purple combination gives a funky modern feel. For maximum impact, use bold blocks of colour; a small floor area can carry off a scarlet vinyl, while the window alcove provides a self-contained space for a splash of purple.

Suite: A white suite in good condition can be adapted to suit any decor. This bath's old brown panelling has been replaced with smooth white-painted MDF boards. The basin also enjoys cleaner lines, with an MDF housing which hides its pedestal and creates storage space. The loo cistern is concealed behind a purple-painted box, and the loo seat has been glammed up with red spray enamel, a pot of glitter and a few coats of polyurethane varnish.

Shower curtain: Make a shower curtain in the colour of your choice using polyurethane-coated nylon. Measure from the rail to just above the bottom of the bath and cut two pieces this length, then sew them together lengthwise. Mark points at 15-20cm intervals, 2.5cm from the top of the curtain. Using an eyelet kit, punch a hole and insert an eyelet at each marked spot. Hang from curtain rings.

The look: Make the smallest room in the house the most colourful – a lick of paint is the key to a low-cost makeover. Add a few decorative accessories to complete your dramatic transformation.

Colour: Strong colour will give a small bathroom a character boost. Mauve and aqua are both contemporary favourites but make an original combination that gives this room an individual look. Cool colours have a less cramping effect than warm, fiery ones, and using the lighter of the two shades on the upper part of the walls helps to maintain an airy atmosphere. Wood panelling can be painted in any colour you like, and usually works out cheaper to buy and install than tiles.

Basin: The big rectangular basin has classic looks, which are complemented by traditional-style taps. Small fittings obviously give you more room to move in tiny bathrooms but larger ones can create an air of luxury. If your heart is set on a generously sized basin, measure up carefully to ensure that there's space for you to stand in front and lean over it comfortably.

Mirror: Large mirrors are excellent for brightening dark rooms, especially if positioned where they can reflect light from the window. They can also help to make a small room feel larger by reflecting the space itself. This unusual wavy design combines practicality with decorative style.

Accessories: The curves of the metal accessories echo the wavy lines of the mirror, from the modern chrome storage trolley to the wall-mounted candleholder which gives the room an air of period charm. Towels continue the colour theme, with a mix of shades from pale green and mauve to deep turquoise.

The look: With soft yellows suggesting sunshine and sand, and distressed cupboard doors reminiscent of weathered driftwood, this tiny bathroom has a seaside flavour. The built-in basin and fitted units create a ship's cabin feel.

Colour: Yellow ensures a sunny atmosphere but, as a warm colour, may make a small room feel tinier, so this scheme balances it with a splashback of fresh white tiles above the bath. Using similar yellows on the walls and cupboards gives the room a streamlined appearance, while the distressed doors create a comfortably lived-in look. Blue accents enrich the scheme by providing a vibrant contrast with the yellow.

Suite: A slipper-shaped bath, which narrows at one end, has improved access to this tiny bathroom. Fitting the semi-recessed basin into cupboard units also makes

efficient use of space. As well as creating storage, it provides a countertop around the basin and conceals its pipework to give a neater look.

Storage: Fitted cupboards maximize storage space in a small bathroom and are invaluable for keeping it neat and tidy. As a cost-effective option, ask a local carpenter to build some, then paint them to match the rest of your decor. For a distressed effect, first apply a dark shade then, when dry, rub candle wax over areas that might suffer wear, such as panel edges. Apply a lighter paint colour and leave to dry, then rub with wire wool to expose patches of base coat.

Floor: As well as having natural good looks and being comfy underfoot, cork is one of the best-value floorcoverings. Buy unfinished tiles and coat with layers of cork tile sealant or hardwearing varnish to seal them for bathroom use.

The look: If you've inherited an all-white bathroom, it shouldn't cost much to smarten it up. You don't have to blast the walls with bright colour – simple designs painted on tiles and flooring give this room its individual look, while clever storage solutions add colour and character.

Colour: A blend of subtle greens and greys takes the clinical edge off the white, creating a relaxed mood that suits the casual style of the furnishings. A mix of tones and textures adds interest – from the forest greens of the tile designs and floor stripes to the olive seersucker curtain and the metallic grey of the galvanized boxes.

Suite: If your budget won't run to an expensive vanity unit or swanky bath surround, why not improvise? Galvanized boxes hide unsightly pipes beneath the basin and provide serious storage capacity, while a seersucker curtain screens the space beneath the bath, which is also used for storage.

Splashback: Green alchemy symbols give a lift to these plain white tiles. If you want to paint tiles already on your wall, practise on spare ones first. Make sure the tiles are clean and dry, then decorate with simple designs using tile paint and an artist's brush.

Floor: Wavy stripes add pattern and colour to the vinyl floor tiles. When decorating vinyl or lino, use a product formulated for these surfaces, as ordinary paints won't stick. For this effect, first paint the floor in cream. When dry, tear the edges off strips of wide masking tape and stick to the floor. Paint a darker shade between the strips. When dry, remove the tape.

BATHROOM TIP
If crumbling grout is spoiling the look of your tiles, remove it carefully using something pointed, such as an old screwdriver. Apply new grout with a small sponge. Work it in well, wipe off excess with a damp sponge, then polish when dry

The look: Choosing a budget suite and inexpensive tiling needn't mean skimping on style. Courageous use of colour can add character to the humblest furnishings. This room gets a retro 1950s feel, with a scheme based on bold black and white.

Colour: Big black and white tiles arranged in chequerboard patterns define the 1950s look, and painting the lower part of the wall black reinforces the colour contrast. Chrome fittings, splashes of hot lipstick pink and a cool pistachio-green door all add to the retro style.

Suite: If you reckon you can't afford new sanitaryware, think again – this classic white suite cost just £200. Bathroom specialists often have budget ranges and give good discounts in sales. You can get especially good deals on discontinued lines or ex-display models. Choose a simple white suite, then add your own style with the rest of the decor.

Tiles: Ceramic wall tiles and vinyl floor tiles in plain colours can be picked up cheaply, yet combining a couple of contrasting colours can create interesting effects. In this small room, a fully chequered splashback might have looked overpowering, but a two-tile-deep border of alternating black and white squares has plenty of impact.

Mirrors: The convex glass in the porthole-style mirrors offers a fish-eye view. The gilt frames have been sprayed with silver paint to match the chrome fittings. These mirrors add to the room's character, while a small extendable model is a more practical addition above the basin.

The look: Painting the walls is the easiest – and cheapest – way to perk up a boring bathroom. If yours seems cold and uninviting, be adventurous – try a deep, warm pink to turn it into a cosy, alluring space.

Colour: Passionate pink not only warms up this room but also gives it a luxurious atmosphere that suits the classic looks of the taps and fittings. The glamorous stone-effect patterning on the wood-panelled bath surround enhances this decadent air. White fittings and tiles set off the darker colours by providing a dazzling contrast.

Suite: The bath and basin have classic styling, with rectangular shaping and 1930s-style moulding around the basin. A paint effect gives the wooden bath surround its stone-effect finish. The chrome-plated taps are also traditional in style, the bath/shower mixer featuring a telephone handset.

Towel shelf: The unusual towel rack can be put together in minutes using a pair of white-painted shelf brackets and a few lengths of rope. Drill holes for the rope along the top of each bracket, and fix them to the wall. Then simply thread the rope through the holes and knot at each end to secure. The decorative brackets suit the classic feel of the room.

Mirrors: Mirrors serve more purposes in a bathroom than you might realize, adding decoration and interest to plain walls. Large mirrors are useful in small bathrooms because they reflect light and space, making the room appear bigger and brighter.

The look: Who says you can't afford a bright new bathroom? Crisp white tiles are amazingly cheap if bought in bulk, and you'll save loads of money if you buy a complete suite rather than individual pieces. Go-with-anything white gives you the freedom to change your colour scheme at any time – simply splash on the paint.

Colour: Brilliant colours not only create their own impact but also form a striking contrast with white. These fittings and tiles look fresh and clean against a sea of cool blue and bands of strong pink. The vertical panels of pink and white act like stripes, leading the eye upwards and adding height to the room.

Suite: The budget suite cost less than £200 from a DIY store but, surrounded by clever colour scheming and design, it looks the business. For a

timeless contemporary look, choose fittings with clean lines and few fussy details, and remember that pure white will always be a winner. If you want to add colour to your bath, build a surround of tongue-and-groove panelling, which you can paint or repaint to match your scheme.

Shelving: Galvanized shelves are sleek, chic and inexpensive. These show how shelving can be arranged creatively to form a stylish design feature. The short shelves add interest to the pink panels, helping them to make a focal point of the basin area.

Floor: Vinyl flooring is cheap, tough, easy to clean and comes in lots of great colours. Sold in sheet or tile form, it is also easy for anyone to lay. Matching the shade to the blue used on the walls boosts this room's colour power even further.

BATHROOM TIP
Remember to budget for plumbing and electrical work – never attempt these jobs yourself. See the Advice section at the back of this book for professional bodies that can supply details of tradesmen in your area

The look: A smart monochrome colour scheme establishes an air of city chic in this elegantly styled bathroom, where the classic good looks of the suite and fittings are inspired by the Edwardian period.

Colour: A combination of black and white is sure to set a distinguished tone. Glossy black wall tiles are offset by the crisp white walls and suite and light chromium taps, while the rich mahogany colour of the loo seat and bath panelling adds a touch of warmth. Elements of pattern give the look a decorative period feel: small black inset tiles enliven the floor area, while the wall tiles are topped off by a narrow border with a traditional geometric design. The grey and white stripes of the Roman blind continue the monochromatic scheme, with only the pictures and soap adding dashes of colour.

Suite: Although the fittings show an Edwardian influence, they are not overfussy in appearance and are scaled to suit the size of modern homes. The basin has a bow front and generous rim, and its curves are echoed in the lid of the loo cistern. The classic-style taps and wood-effect loo seat and bath panelling also evoke a traditional feel.

Window: Neater than curtains but providing an opportunity to introduce patterned fabric, a Roman blind is the perfect choice of window treatment for this smart but dressy scheme. Stripes work well with this type of blind as they complement the straight lines of the pleats. If you want to make a blind using your own fabric, look for a kit that includes all the fittings – it's easier than buying them separately and also provides full instructions.

BATHROOM TIP
A modern radiator detracts from the look of a period-style room, so seek out a traditional design. Specialist radiator companies and some bathroom suppliers stock them, or you could try salvage yards for genuine period fittings

The look: Rustic simplicity meets classic splendour in this comfortable scheme, where a magnificent slipper bath makes a strong style statement amid a reassuring environment of unassuming colours and natural textures.

Colour: Walls in soft cream, plus wood panelling painted in a gentle sage green, give this room its relaxed country feel, which is enhanced by the natural tone and texture of the seagrass flooring. Against this calming backdrop, the black and white colouring of the bath boldly asserts its classic contours and ensures that it is seen as a dramatic focal point.

Bath: With one end curving up to provide a luxurious headrest, a slipper bath makes an even more impressive sight than a standard roll-top. If you have the space, place it in the centre of the room to show off its shapely lines and ornamental feet. As traditional freestanding baths have no surrounding surfaces, a bath rack is essential for holding soaps and washing items – look for one with a finish that matches your taps.

Floor: Seagrass and other natural floorcoverings create a comfortably rustic look, although their prickly fibres are not so kind to bare feet. Like normal carpeting, most types will not wear well in damp conditions, but can be used with care if backed with rubber. Coir matting is the most practical choice as its fibres benefit from being kept moist.

Accessories: The wall print and the selection of patterned tiles add touches of decorative detail while blending in with the subtle colours of the background. The white-painted wooden stool and towel rail have traditional country looks, and the leafy pot plant also adds to the natural feel.

la chambre turque

The look: A mix of influences have had a hand in this cosy bathroom, which brims with decorative detail. Yellow checked wallpaper and a soft blue carpet create a comfortable country-house atmosphere, while Chinese-style plates and a Moroccan-inspired alcove add a more exotic touch.

Colour: The yellow and white checks of the wallpaper fill the room with cheerful pattern and sunny colour, creating a fresh, country feel. Blue enriches the scheme by forming a vibrant contrast. Choosing a deep-coloured carpet adds a sense of comfort to the room, while using blue to pick out the alcove focuses attention on its shape. Colour unites accessories as varied as the Moroccan lantern and oriental plates, which all feature similar shades of blue.

Suite: The distinctive scalloped detailing of the suite strikes a chord with the room's

decorative character, while the wood tones of the maple-effect bath panelling and loo seat enhance its country charm. The classic pillar taps are chromium plated.

Storage and display:
The alcove provides an eye-catching display space. Its arched shape and intricately patterned shelf edgings point to Moroccan inspiration, perhaps suggested by the beaten metal lantern. The shelf trims are flat MDF mouldings, available from good timber merchants in a range of patterns. They are glued in place and painted in a lighter shade of blue to make them stand out against the background. The wall around the recess is edged with braid, glued on and decorated with small chair studs. The blue and white plates have been arranged in a shape that echoes the arch of the alcove, with the pot given pride of place on a painted wooden corbel in the centre.

BATHROOM TIP
Choose a vinyl wallpaper for a bathroom. Vinyl finishes are designed to withstand damp and condensation, so will last longer than other papers

The look: Purify your senses in a bathroom designed to wash the day away. Powdery pastels have just enough colour power to refresh a sleepy mind. Together with a sculptural suite, flowing fabrics and ice-cool flooring, they create a totally cleansing environment.

Colour: Pale but interesting shades are what gives this beautifully feminine scheme its character. Choose colours rather than bland neutrals, but maintain a light touch, with cool grey-green and ice-blue for walls and floor, and pretty pinks and yellows for other furnishings and towels. Areas of shine and sparkle in glass and Perspex accessories help to create a feeling of space and light. The vinyl flooring, which resembles tiny squares of glass, also has a shimmering, reflective quality that enhances the bright, clean feel of the scheme.

Bath: The old-fashioned elegance of the furnishings prevents the look from feeling overly clinical. The pink-painted roll-top bath, with elaborate feet picked out in white, looks twice as glamorous when draped with a flowing shower curtain. Hung from an oval rail fixed to the ceiling, the yellow curtain is deliberately overlong so that it swirls lavishly across the floor.

Basin: A painted console table with graceful curved legs serves as a washstand for the bowl-style basin, which is a modern take on a Victorian design. The taps are wall-mounted onto a splashback of hexagonal mosaic tiles.

Accessories: A Perspex shelf stacked with mock medical vessels in clear glass boosts the hygiene appeal, while a decorative candle chandelier sets a more romantic mood. A laundry bag in a pink and yellow floral print makes a pretty hideaway for bits and pieces not smart enough to put on show.

The look: A mood of cool restfulness pervades this room, thanks to cloudy blue-washed walls complemented by floaty sheer curtains and the graceful details of a classic-style suite and splashback.

Colour: The blue colourwash is a beautifully subtle way of filling the room with colour while maintaining a light and airy feel. Its shades are echoed by the splashback tiles, where soft blue inset and border tiles form a gentle contrast to the plain white squares. The natural wood tones of the flooring, bath panel and toilet seat help to warm up the cool scheme, while ceramics in intense blues strengthen it with accents of exotic Mediterranean colour.

Suite: Fancy stepped mouldings around bowl and pedestal bases give the suite its classic looks, while the wood-effect loo seat and bath panelling also denote traditional style. The taps feature easy-to-use lever controls with a period design.

Splashback: Laying plain tiles diagonally gives them an individual look, and these have small blue insets to add further decorative interest. The border of blue pencil tiles provides definition between the white splashback and pale colourwash, and evokes a period feel by mimicking a dado rail.

Radiator: Despite adding warmth and comfort, modern radiators often have a cold, functional appearance. Painting them in a colour can help; use radiator paint or apply multi-surface primer beneath a gloss or eggshell top coat. Ensure the radiator is cold before you start.

The look: Soak away your cares amid the genteel atmosphere of an Edwardian bathroom, as you gaze up at your art collection from the comfort of a hand-painted roll-top bath!

Colour: The scheme is inspired by the colours of the bath, which is painted with a Florentine design in cobalt blue and golden yellow. The lighter blue that covers the walls has an uplifting, summery feel but is intense enough to make an impact in this high-ceilinged room. The smooth wooden flooring tones with the yellow to add warmth, while the white woodwork, suite and curtains provide a fresh contrast for the deeper colours.

Suite: The roll-top bath is a newly manufactured interpretation of a traditional design. A large freestanding bath like this requires space to show off its impressive curves so, if possible, place it in the centre of the room to form a dramatic focal point. The basin, loo and bidet would fit most rooms; although they have the lines of traditional fired clay fittings, they are contemporary in scale and proportion. Gold-plated taps and a mahogany-effect loo seat enhance their elegant looks.

Window: White lace is a sure winner if you want a touch of old world charm, and will give your windows a beautifully dressed look without shutting out light. Make it into gathered curtains, and tie back loosely at the sides for a look of pure indulgent romance.

Accessories: Don't save paintings and ornaments for bedrooms and living rooms – a period-style bathroom does justice to sumptuous accessories. Search junk shops and antiques stores for decorative mirrors, and don't worry if the frames are slightly battered – they will add a fashionable air of shabby chic.

BATHROOM TIP
A large cast-iron bath can be very heavy when filled with water and bathers, so check before investing in one that your floor will be able to take the strain

The look: The original 1930s tiles on the walls inspired a slightly Art Deco flavour for this smart bathroom. An abundance of white keeps the mood bright and airy, while traditional fittings and chequerboard floor tiles add to the period feel.

Colour: Decorating both the walls and ceiling in white creates a clean and sparkling atmosphere as well as a fantastic sense of space. Light bounces off the white surfaces, especially the glossy wall tiles, to make the room seem bigger and brighter. This plain, pale background lends greater impact to the period elements of the room – the narrow strips of green 1930s tiling stand out against the sea of white, while the bold black and white tiles put the focus firmly on the floor.

Suite: A suite with straight lines, angular shaping and traditional-style taps is in tune with the 1930s feel. The deep bath is boxed in with wooden panels: the long one features a raised design reminiscent of Art Deco patterns, while the hinged end panel opens like a door to allow space inside to be used for storage.

Mirrors: Set way up on the walls, the long mirrors may be a bit too high for comfortable use, but their prime purpose is to make the room feel wider by reflecting light and space. Placing two directly opposite each other is particularly effective. The small extendable mirror wall-mounted above the basin serves for shaving or applying cosmetics.

Towel rail: With a gleaming chrome finish that matches the taps, the simple towel rail is positioned just above the radiator so that its heat keeps the towels warm and dry.

The look: The Romans made a cult of bathtimes, so borrow a bit of their design style for a bathroom full of classical chic. Mosaic-effect flooring and splashback tiles handpainted with large Roman numerals set the theme.

Colour: Plain cream walls and textured floor tiles in a similar shade suggest the sun-bleached surfaces of a Roman villa, and give the large room a wonderfully bright and airy atmosphere. Picking out the woodwork and shelves in white helps to enhance the richness of the cream, giving it a softer feel, while the golden glow of the taps and other fittings introduces a hint of glamour. Orange border tiles add interest to the large floor area and characterful detail to the scheme, with their pattern based on an original Romanesque rope design.

Suite: A roll-top bath with elaborate sculptural feet, a basin with a pillar-like pedestal and an old-fashioned loo with a high-level cistern have classic good looks the Romans would have appreciated. The flush pipe and pull chain of the loo have a gleaming brass finish that matches the taps.

Accessories: The glitzy golden highlights continue with a classy set of practical accessories, including tooth-brush holders, a wall-mounted shelf and towel hooks and a stunning round mirror frame. A themed look relies on details to make it work and, like the numerals painted on the splashback tiles, the classic-style shelf corbels give a definite nod towards Roman style. These three shelves also offer a display area for evocative accessories such as a plaster head and pillar.

The look: Regency stripes get an up-to-date twist with fresh, invigorating colours, unleashing a burst of modern energy in a room based around a traditional-style suite and accessories.

Colour: While the jazzy pattern and enlivening colours of the stripes create a refreshing atmosphere, the glossy white tiles and glass shower screen brighten the look even further by reflecting light from the window. Green towels and cream-coloured candles echo the colours of the stripes.

Walls: The wall stripes are deliberately uneven, their slightly wavy edges giving a less regimental effect than clean-cut lines. First paint the entire wall with cream, then measure out the stripes and mark them on lightly with pencil, using a plumbline to get them straight. Paint on the green stripes freehand, using an artist's brush for the narrow ones. It doesn't matter if your coverage is slightly uneven as this will only add to the casual, contemporary effect.

Suite: Boxing in the bath with clean white tiles plays down the classic character of the suite, but it makes itself felt through details such as the wood-effect loo seat and gold-plated taps. The shower rose is also traditional in style; if you choose a fixed shower head like this, make sure you place it at the correct height so that all family members can stand upright beneath it. You will also need a shower screen to catch splashes – this glass model features a decorative etched design.

Towel rails: Two towel rails provide ample hanging space. A simple gold-plated bar allows towels to hang over the radiator, while a freestanding wooden rack also keeps them warm and dry when placed in front of it.

The look: A Victorian roll-top bath teams up with pretty painted bowls and other decorative accessories to create a bathroom with an air of old-fashioned charm. A restrained neutral colour scheme sets the scene.

Colour: Rustic stone flooring and wood-panelled walls painted in a rich cream give the room a traditional country-cottage feel. The cool blue-grey paintwork on the bath sets a slightly more sophisticated tone, while enhancing the relaxing atmosphere.

Wall panelling: Wood panelling is a popular choice of wall cover for classic or country-style bathrooms, and is ideal for concealing the less-than-perfect surfaces often found in older homes. Tongue-and-groove boards, widely available from DIY stores, are easy to install and can be painted in a colour that matches your scheme. After painting, apply clear matt varnish to make the boards water-resistant, as damp can cause the wood to warp.

Suite: For any bathroom that aims to evoke classic comfort, a roll-top bath is a necessity. These large, cast-iron tubs originated in the nineteenth century but many bathroom dealers now offer authentic-looking, lightweight repro-ductions. This room's taps and small round wash basin also have a period look.

Accessories: Further old-fashioned glamour is added by the gilt-framed mirror and the chandelier reflected in it. Ceramic bowls decorated with pink and yellow flowers add accents of brighter colour.

The look: Wallow in nostalgia with a look that's pure Art Deco. Patterned tiles and polished chrome fittings set the style for this flamboyantly luxurious bathroom, while photos and ornaments in the style of the era add perfect finishing touches.

Colour: Pale lavender walls provide a chic backdrop for an otherwise monochrome scheme. A border of tiles at picture rail height adds classic proportions to the room, and the cream paintwork on the wall above echoes the floor tiles, which are enlivened by small black inserts. The Art Deco designs of the wall tiles are a key element in defining the look, and their jazzy patterns are offset by the plain black bath surround. A few pale green towels and floral-print accessories add subtle colour accents to soften the angularity of the scheme.

Suite: The geometric shape of this sleek suite lends itself to Art Deco style, and the chrome-plated taps also evoke a retro feel. The black bath panel creates a smart contrast with the white fittings.

Wall tiles: You don't need many patterned tiles to make a style statement, so it's worth spending a bit more on luxurious designs that really say what you want them to. Distinctive tiles like these are best used sparingly – just one or two rows as a splashback above bath or basin will get the message across.

Accessories: The Art Deco influence continues with slick and shapely chrome accessories, such as the oval mirror and round wall lamps. The lithe, energetic bathing girls portrayed in the ornament and prints encapsulate the feelgood factor of the era.

The look: Classic chic gives a nod to contemporary cool, with a traditionally styled suite and flowing curtains looking to the past, while a steely combination of dark greys and white join with shiny chrome accessories to add a striking modern edge.

Colour: This monochrome scheme sets a smart and sophisticated tone, and the grey paint shades complement the metallic gleam of the chrome furnishings. Dark grey walls could easily overwhelm a small room, but when balanced with plenty of fresh white they create a striking impact in this large, light-filled space. Using two shades as wall stripes introduces a subtle touch of tonal variation to soften the strident white and grey contrast.

Walls: Stripes in closely toning shades add interest to an extensive wall area and help to break up the intensity of the colour without lessening its impact. Vertical stripes are also useful for increasing the illusion of height in a room. To get them straight, hang a plumbline from the top of the wall and mark on the stripes with pencil lines. Use low-tack tape to mask off each colour, and let the paint dry before removing it to ensure a clean edge.

Suite: Fittings with classic styling give the room its air of old-fashioned chic. The curves of the roll-top bath are echoed by the rounded front and pedestal of the basin. Painting the bath to match the walls links the two strongest features of the look.

Accessories: Long sheer curtains add another classic touch to soften the scheme, but are plain enough to complement more modern elements such as the sleek storage cabinet and other chrome fittings which fill the room with high-shine glamour.

BATHROOM TIP
Although sheer curtains provide privacy by day, they won't preserve your modesty when the lights go on after dark. Add a roller blind, fitted within the window recess, which can be concealed behind a decorative heading when rolled up

The look: Old-fashioned fittings and silver-painted floorboards bring an air of subtle glamour to this small bathroom, while accessories lend the look an oriental flavour.

Colour: The walls are covered in a colourwash-effect paper in a pale neutral shade, which creates a light but calming backdrop for the small space. White woodwork and fittings freshen the overall look, while shiny silver floorboards also help to brighten up the room and increase the feeling of space by reflecting light. Their luxurious sheen is echoed by the gleam of the chrome-plated taps. The window blind and leafy plant offset the pale colours with darker accents of brown and green.

Suite: The plain white finish of the roll-top bath suits the simple styling of the room, while its gold-painted feet add just a hint of decadence.

Its traditional looks are complemented by the chunky pedestal basin, with its classic square lines and moulded detailing. The taps and telephone-style shower mixer are also traditional in design.

Floor: While a glitzy paint effect might look overdone if used to cover the walls, a small floor area can add just the right amount of sparkle to glam up a tiny room. To give wooden floorboards a silvery finish, apply a metallic paint or multi-purpose enamel that's suitable for use on wood. When dry, protect the paintwork with two coats of floor varnish for a durable, waterproof surface.

Accessories: The bamboo ladder, woven paper blind and exotic potted palm all add character by introducing a touch of oriental style. The ladder not only looks decorative but also makes an excellent towel rail.

The look: A freestanding bath draped with shower curtains is the focal point of this romantically elegant Georgian-style scheme. Decorated in watery greens, with floral fabrics and gleaming gold accessories, this bathroom is unashamedly luxurious but also perfectly practical.

Colour: If you want a room that's both colourful and relaxing, go for green. A soft shade creates a reassuring feel but also makes a refreshing foil for rich gold details and floral designs. Painting the walls above the picture rail in cool cream also maintains an airy atmosphere. A darker green adds definition to the bath, while a neutral carpet provides a calming base.

Suite: The bath and console basin have beautifully old-fashioned looks but are recent manufactures. Whereas genuine period pieces often require restoration, brand-new lookalikes combine modern quality with classic character. Like original designs, the bath is made of cast iron. You can paint the white base in any colour to match your scheme, and a touch of gold leaf will give the claw feet a glitzy finish.

Taps and shower: The taps also combine modern technology with traditional style, their brass finish complementing the room's gold accessories. The swan-necked shower riser and fixed rose provide a more thorough soak than a hand-held mixer attachment, and long, gathered shower curtains add to the scheme's air of romance.

Accessories: Go all out for glamour with gilded accessories, such as the towel rail, candlestick and mirror frame. Or, if you find their lavish leaf and flower designs a bit too ornate, add a lighter touch of romance using pretty perfume bottles, a jug of fresh flowers and white cotton towels with a hint of embroidery.

BATHROOM TIP
Glam up wooden mirror frames and the claw feet of baths using a gilding kit, available from craft stores. It includes metallic leaf to give a golden finish, plus the glue and tools required to apply it

The look: A suite with sassy angles and a colour scheme based on soft sea shades brings flirty 1930s style to a standard-sized bathroom. Subtle use of Art Deco patterns and accessories helps to create the look without overpowering the room.

Colour: With a splashback of white tiles, and a pale shade of aqua adding the merest hint of colour to the walls, the pale backdrop keeps the room feeling light and spacious, forming a cool foil for the stronger colours of the features that give it character. The flooring grounds the scheme with a sharper green, and helps draw attention to the Art Deco border tiles by echoing one of their colours. Black accents smarten up the look, and a striking green frame makes a focal point of the mirror.

Suite: The angular lines of the loo and basin are reminiscent of the geometric patterns associated with Art Deco style. The bath carries a more direct reference, with the design on its panelling specially cut to echo the fan motif of the border tiles. The chrome-plated taps feature up-to-date lever controls but with traditional styling.

Floor: The floor is tiled with Marmoleum, a healthy, eco-friendly covering made from natural raw materials. Available in many colours and designs, it has a smooth surface that stops dirt and water from penetrating and discourages house dust mites.

Accessories: Sparkling chrome and glass accessories are a must for 1930s glamour. The sleek storage trolley displays a good-sized shaving or make-up mirror and a set of antique perfume bottles from that era, while the wall lamps that flank the mirror are also authentic Art Deco pieces.

The look: In this light, elegant scheme, an elaborately styled suite and glamorous gold accessories benefit from an ultra-simple background. With the walls and flooring kept perfectly plain, they work their own magic to create a romantic but classy look.

Colour: Cream provides a versatile, space-enhancing backdrop for many styles of decor. Some people feel reluctant to team a white suite with cream walls, but they work well together as the contrast makes the cream feel richer and warmer, while boosting the fresh, clean appeal of the fittings. The pale blue paint of the bath injects a dash of subtle colour, while the wooden flooring and furniture add a comforting touch of natural warmth.

Suite: If you like the idea of a romantic bathroom, have fun with fittings and search out the fanciest you can find. Although roll-top baths are now widely available, a highly decorative basin may be more difficult to track down. However, you could try adding white-painted trelliswork panels to the sides of a large traditional design. A loo with high-level cistern completes the old-fashioned line-up, while the gold-plated flush pipe and taps add a feeling of opulence.

Furniture: If you've space for it, occasional furniture will give a bathroom a comfier, lived-in look. This simple wooden chair and table provide a contrast in style that helps to highlight the ornate design of the suite.

Accessories: Wall-mounted accessories keep basin tops clear of clutter, add attractive finishing touches and give a bathroom a well-equipped feel. Look for fittings that match your taps – the shelf brackets, soap dish and tumbler holders enhance this room's luxurious golden glimmer.

The look: Black and white tiling combines a Victorian bathhouse feel with the impact of a bold modern colour scheme. An eclectic mix of old and new furnishings reflects the two sides of its character – from the traditional roll-top bath to contemporary glass shelves and groovy rubber flooring.

Colour: Black and white is not a relaxing combination for rooms where you spend a lot of time, but in a bathroom it can look smart and striking, and is a classic choice if you want a more masculine style. Big chequerboard wall tiles and black flooring make a dramatic statement. To soften the starkness of the monochrome scheme, the bath is painted in a warmer chocolate brown and the upper walls in a light mustard. The picture lifts the look with small splashes of brighter colour – it's made up of pieces of towelling glued to white card.

Suite: The roll-top bath has traditional shaping but relatively simple feet, and, painted in a business-like brown, fits in well with the somewhat austere appeal of the room. The basin combines cleaner, more contemporary lines with classic-style taps.

Storage: The old trolley has the practical plus points of a contemporary storage system – deep trays with plenty of space for towels and toiletries, and castors that make it easy to wheel around. Its battered metal finish forms a relaxed contrast with slick modern storage features such as the glass shelf and galvanized metal box.

Floor: Rubber flooring is fashionable, hardwearing and water-resistant, and this studded design provides an anti-slip surface. It is available in sheet or tile form in many different colours, but is more expensive than vinyl or lino.

The look: Re-create the feel of an old Italian villa using easy-to-achieve paint effects and characterful fittings. With sun-baked browns, olive greens and wooden shutters, all you need is a ray or two of Tuscan sunshine to complete the picture.

Colour: The earthy terracotta on the walls and the rich reddish-brown floor tiles create a warm glow, especially when bathed in sunlight from the window. The heat is tempered by a mix of cool but traditional greens, from the deep jade of the chair to the soft olive used on all the woodwork.

Paint effects: A terracotta colourwash gives the walls a natural, textural appearance. Apply a pale colour, such as cream, and leave to dry. Then dilute a terracotta shade with water until you get the strength you want, and apply using a wide brush and crisscross strokes. The distressed effect on the wood panelling and shutters evokes an air of faded grandeur. First paint the wood with a terracotta shade, then rub candlewax over areas that might suffer wear, such as panel edges. Add a coat of light green, then, when dry, rub back with wire wool to expose patches of the base coat.

Suite: Any sanitaryware that looks as if it has a history would sit well here. The farmhouse-style sink, with its decorative spray of ivy leaves, fits in perfectly with this classic country style, and a wood-clad cistern gives the loo an individual look.

Window: Shutters give the room a continental appearance. This window is dressed with solid panels that fold back neatly to let in maximum light. The shaped pediment that tops the window adds an ornate finishing touch.

The look: This laid-back look exudes an air of faded glamour, with a mixture of old furniture and a tarnished gold paint effect on the bath. Off-white walls and painted floorboards form a serene backdrop.

Colour: A mix of soft neutrals and natural textures creates a comfortable atmosphere, and using the same shade on the walls and floor makes for a particularly relaxing look. The matt gold finish on the bath tones with the gentle browns of the wooden furniture. The cream chest blends with the walls and floor while adding interest with subtle woven texture. Green and blue accents, featuring in the stool seat, book cover and bath design on the mirror, introduce the merest hint of colour.

Bath: The roll-top bath came from a salvage yard, which was full of original fittings and sanitaryware rescued from period homes. See your local phone book to find your nearest yard. As long as an old bath is in good condition, you can decorate it to suit your scheme – the outside of this one has been spruced up with a mixture of gold powder and matt varnish, which gives an aged, tarnished finish. Gold-plated taps complete the glamorous transformation.

Furniture: Old furniture adds character to a bathroom and can be just as functional as purpose-designed modern pieces. This room is home to a medley of junk-shop finds. The Lloyd Loom chest with padded lift-up lid doubles as a comfy seat and laundry basket. Every bathroom needs a mirror, and a classic design propped casually on a stool suits this lived-in look. The bath motif on its top panel adds the perfect finishing touch.

BATHROOM TIP
Don't keep wooden furniture too near baths and basins as water splashes can damage waxed surfaces. Give it a good polish to protect it from the steamy bathroom atmosphere

The look: If there's always a queue for the bathroom in the mornings, decorate with bright red. It stimulates a sense of urgency, so will get people in and out fast. This room offsets its striking colour scheme with more traditional fittings and furnishings.

Colour: A strong scarlet used as a flat, solid wall colour is sure to make an impact. Teaming it with plenty of white prevents it from overwhelming a small room, and also adds extra energy by creating a dazzling contrast. Here red and white are equally balanced, with both colours used on the walls and then played off against each other in a more lively fashion in the chequerboard floor tiles. Yellow accents help to temper the strong contrast while adding a third cheerful colour to the mix.

Basin: The flowing curves of the pedestal basin are easy on the eye, a shapely contrast with the bold geometric effect of the floor tiles. Tall pillar taps complement its classic styling.

Furniture: The white-painted wooden drawer unit also features elegant curved detailing, and the wooden chair adds a relaxed natural touch amid the strong colours. While the open shelves of the drawer unit keep toiletries and towels easily accessible, a family bathroom also needs a wall-mounted cabinet, preferably with lockable door, to keep medicines out of reach of small children.

Floor: Combining vinyl or lino tiles in different colours is an easy way of adding enlivening pattern to your bathroom. Vinyl is easy to lay yourself, but make sure that the floor surface is even before you start. Linoleum is more expensive than most vinyls and should be laid by a professional fitter.

The look: Dark wood panelling set amongst simple white walls gives this bathroom the air of a traditional gentleman's club. A suite with distinctive rope-design mouldings sets the seal on the look of sophisticated grandeur.

Colour: The rich colour of the solid cherrywood flooring and the darker tones of the mahogany-effect bath panel give the room a warm, comfortable atmosphere, while contrasting them with plain white walls keeps the look clean and unfussy. The set of monochrome pictures in simple black frames enhances the smart, masculine feel, and any additional colour accents are limited to neutral shades, such as the camel-coloured towel.

Suite: The rope-twist moulding around the bath and column-like pedestals, and the arch rim detail on the basin give this suite its distinctive traditional looks. The taps feature an interesting mixture of chromium and light-gold finishes.

Wall panelling: The panelled effect on the wall behind the bath has been created using strips of MDF, which are decorated with a wood-effect paint technique in a colour that matches the flooring. DIY stores and craft shops stock graining kits which include the paints and tools you need to create a convincing wood grain finish. These panels frame a large mirror, which helps to increase the illusion of space.

Accessories: The gallery of photographs adds personality to this simple scheme, and their subject matter – portraits of film stars – injects an air of glamour. Arranging them side by side around the walls not only breaks up the expanse of plain white but also adds a sense of order to the room.

The look: As this room shows, colour and creative accessorizing can pull even the tiniest bathroom out of the doldrums. An unusual mix of mellow shades sets the mood for an offbeat look, while decorative accessories and shelving add character.

Colour: With warm yellow offset by cool mauve and fresh aqua, none of the key colours is strong enough to overpower the tiny space, but they create a lively look when used together. More colour is included as accents – in the deep pink and orange towels and the lime green candles. The flowers of the shower curtain echo the wall colours.

Mosaic tiles: Ideal for creating a trendy splashback, mosaic tiling can help to bring a jaded bathroom back to life. To make it easy to cover large areas, mosaic tiles can be bought attached to backing sheets. Apply adhesive to the tiled side and stick to the wall. When dry, carefully peel off the backing sheet and grout the tiles in the normal way.

Shelves: You don't need expensive fitted cupboards to keep your bathroom tidy. The trelliswork shelving units fit in well with the mood of the room and look pretty even when packed with run-of-the-mill toiletries, yet they were a bargain buy from a local shop.

Accessories: Treat your bathroom as you would any other room in the house, by adding character with pictures and ornaments. Decorative items and a collection of candles add to the relaxed, romantic feel of this room.

BATHROOM TIP
Turn a wooden loo seat into a work of art using coloured images cut from wrapping paper or magazines. Sand the seat, brush on PVA adhesive and, when tacky, stick the images on top. Leave to dry, then apply a coat of clear varnish

The look: If you want to achieve that sea-fresh feeling, you can't go wrong with cool blues. A few coloured furnishings against a backdrop of white are all that's needed for a shipshape modern look.

Colour: A fail-safe method of room scheming is to use a single colour in many different shades, from light to dark, throughout your room. This idea works particularly well with blues, which need only the addition of white to lift the look. In this room, white is used in abundance to create a fresh atmosphere, while the blues feature in smaller amounts – from the navy flooring to the cobalt-painted bath panel to the light aquas in the band of mosaic tiles that punctuates the white-tiled wall. Like the tiles, the loo seat brings together both light and dark shades and adds lively pattern to the scheme.

Suite: The basin and loo have classic Art Deco styling and traditional taps, but replacing the original loo seat with a quirky fish-patterned design has added a touch of individuality. The bath is panelled with tongue-and-groove boards, painted in a blue that matches the shower curtain.

Radiator: The radiator provides another opportunity to add colour to the room. Try to use a special radiator paint or, if you can't find one in the colour you want, apply a coat of multi-surface primer followed by your chosen colour in oil-based gloss or eggshell. Make sure the radiator is cold before you start painting.

Mirror: Choose a mirror with a plain wooden frame, and you can paint it to match your colour scheme. Use a wood-stain if you want the grain to remain visible.

The look: The best bathrooms combine function with flair, and a touch of individual style can make all the difference. In this room, classic elements, quirky accessories and theatrical colour make a stimulating mix.

Colour: Walls covered in deep Mediterranean blue create a dramatic atmosphere, and an electrifying contrast comes from accents of bright pink, inspired by the pink plastic bath toy. Using pink to highlight the skirting and dado rail enhances the classic flavour of the scheme. The white-painted floorboards and sheer curtains provide a touch of light relief, and the aqua green of the mirror unit also makes a fresh contrast for the dark walls. White and pink come together in the woven chair and laundry basket.

Suite: The roll-top bath is complemented by traditional taps. For an even more decorative look, paint the base of the bath in a colour to match your room scheme, using water-resistant paint. This room also features a classic pedestal basin, again with traditional tap controls.

Accessories: Don't stop at toothbrush holders and soap dishes – adding a few arty extras can make your bathroom into a place where you want to spend some time. Stamp your own style on the room with pictures or wall ornaments. Mirrors can also provide decorative opportunities – look for unusual shapes or frames, or period-style designs such as the Art Deco mirror and shelf unit above the basin.

The look: With mosaic tiles covering the walls, bath surround and floor, this bathroom is a real labour of love – the effect is easy to achieve but does take time.

Colour: Pure white clears the senses to give this room its spartan charm, which is emphasized by the natural textures of the accessories. The mosaic patterning adds subtle interest to the white surfaces, and its irregular shaping gives an individual look. The blue wave adds a single splash of eye-catching colour which is dramatic in its simplicity.

Tiles: Irregularly shaped mosaics can be created by smashing up ceramic wall tiles. Place a few in a thick plastic bag and secure the top. Wearing safety goggles, tap with a hammer to break the tiles. Using a craft knife, score the surface you want to cover to give a key, then draw on a design with pencil. Lay the tile pieces within your design lines and cut to shape with tile nippers if necessary. Stick them down by applying waterproof PVA glue or tile adhesive to your surface. When all the tiles have set, mix and apply waterproof grout following the maker's instructions. When dry, polish up the mosaic with a soft cloth.

Accessories: The collection of unusual accessories puts some soul into the room. The hand-crafted rosewood corner cabinet depicts the tree of life, while a pagan wand leans against the wall. The shells and driftwood scattered across the floor are natural finds picked up around the world. A candle in the corner and a sprinkling of rose petals on the water promise a magical bathtime experience.

The look: Create a rainforest in your bathroom! Lush, leafy plants, a floor strewn with logs and pebbles, and tribal masks gazing down over the bath make for a truly exotic watering-hole.

Colour: Let the natural world be your guide, and base your scheme on the earthy browns and natural textures of wood and stone. White walls freshen the overall look, while the large, sand-coloured floor tiles used for the bath splashback soften the contrast between light and dark. The leafy greens of the plants and the deep blues of the bath and mosaic tiles add accents of colour to lift the neutral palette.

Suite: The bath and loo are from a reclamation yard, which is a good source of cheap fittings. Dark blue paint on the base and a copper finish on the feet make the bath look as if it was made for the room, while the loo has been given a new wooden seat. The cistern and exposed pipework is boxed in with plywood and covered in varnished willow screening.

Shower: A white curtain above the unusual round shower base stops water from soaking the room. The iron shower ring, made by a local blacksmith, hangs from a hook in the ceiling.

Floor: The dark tones of the terracotta floor tiles are perfect for an exotic look. Bring the jungle theme alive with varnished tree-trunk slices and smooth pebbles arranged around the bath, plus huge potted palms which thrive in a steamy atmosphere.

The look: Minimalist chic meets classic splendour in this light-filled bathroom, where a traditional roll-top bath with gleaming silver feet takes centre stage against a backdrop of pure white tiles.

Colour: White equals bright, and the effect is dazzling when it is used on both walls and floor. Brick-shaped wall tiles give a less monotonous look than square ones, and painting the upper part of the walls blue provides welcome colour interest. It also helps to improve the proportions of the room by appearing to lower the high ceiling. The band of mosaic tiles, repeated along the windowsill, adds an element of smart but subtle pattern to relieve the plainness of the walls.

Bath: The simple colour scheme unites the old and new elements of the room, with the bath painted in the same bright blue as the walls, and its elaborate silver feet

and traditional chrome taps echoing the sleek finish of the modern trolley. Metallic paint will give a silvery finish on claw feet, but a more luxurious shine can easily be achieved using silver or aluminium leaf. This should be applied using a special glue called size, and finished with shellac varnish – ask your craft store for advice on gilding techniques.

Storage: In this pared-down scheme, a mobile storage trolley takes on a multipurpose role as towel holder, mirror support and toiletry store. Most bathrooms also need cupboard space to achieve a clean, minimalist look.

Window: Wooden shutters provide a stylish window treatment with a continental or period flavour, and can be painted in any colour. Solid shutters provide total privacy when closed, while louvred ones have slats that can be adjusted to let in varying degrees of light.

The look: The bold colours and textures of a lush tropical landscape mix well with 'weathered' metals to create this striking modern bathroom. Leafy green plants and wicker accessories emphasize the natural, organic look.

Colour: The stunning grass green on the walls forms a vibrant contrast with the dull metals of the bath panel and candleholder, offsetting their hard-edged industrial style with energizing colour. It also determines the natural theme of the scheme, which is continued with the woven textures and neutral tones of the sisal-effect flooring, wicker chair and seagrass storage basket. The deeper greens of the leafy plants bring out the tropical feel, while the towels and bath mat lift the look with accents of pale green, yellow and pink.

Metallics: The bath panels and splashback are covered in pre-weathered zinc titanium alloy, and the dramatically tall candleholder has a similar finish. The galvanized metal cabinet and plant pots balance these dark greys with their lighter colour, but their matt surfaces reinforce the stark, natural feel of the look. The only real shine comes from the traditionally styled chrome-plated bath/shower mixer.

Storage: The wall-mounted storage cabinet combines the advantages of a closed cupboard with the ability to keep items in easy view. The lockable door means that toiletries and medicines can be stored out of the reach of children, but the mesh front allows you to see at a glance what's inside.

Floor: The flooring looks like woven sisal but is in fact a realistic vinyl lookalike. While adding convincing tone and texture, it is a more practical choice for a bathroom than most genuine natural floorcoverings.

The look: Get each day off to a bright start with a blast of brilliant Caribbean colour. Multicoloured stripes and blocks of vivid primary hues create a fun, carnival atmosphere in this small bathroom.

Colour: Hardly a colour in the spectrum has been left out, but the key shades are chosen for maximum impact, with bold blue, yellow and orangey-red covering the entire room to form a vibrantly contrasting mix. Used to paint the wooden floorboards, wall panelling and bath surround, the deep blue grounds the scheme and creates a dark foil for the jazzy stripes of the loo and rug. Yellow fills the room with Caribbean sunshine, while the blue star-stencilled ceiling suggests tropical skies. The red-painted walls and accents of sea green on the window and door frames add punch with further exotic colour.

Suite: Traditionally shaped fittings and taps complement the decorative character of the room. Painting the bath panelling blue makes it blend in with the walls and floor, while decorating the loo has turned it into an eye-catching focal point. The multicoloured stripes on its base and the spotted design on its seat were applied using enamel paints, which are available in small tins.

Accessories: The inspiration for the room scheme came from the toilet-roll holder, which was made in the West Indies from an old oil drum. Other ethnic-style accessories, such as the tribal heads on the wall and the simple metal candle sconce, enhance the dazzling Caribbean theme, while the tropical-style bath mat and fish dangling from the mobile echo the room's fun, zingy colours.

BATHROOM TIP
Some paint manufacturers offer kitchen and bathroom ranges specially formulated for steamy rooms. Designed to resist moisture and inhibit mildew growth, they also give a wipe-clean finish

The look: If you want a colourful look but are short of inspiration, a fabric can make a good starting point. This palette of rainbow hues is based on colours featured in the window blind, which is framed by a dramatic curved pelmet to form the focal point of this offbeat scheme.

Colour: The bathroom is one place where you can have fun with colour. Melon-pink walls form a vibrant contrast with shades of blue and purple, and the mix of reds and pinks jostling together below dado level makes this small bathroom anything but boring. The tiles and mirror frame have been painted to fit the scheme.

Suite: Choosing a classic white suite leaves you free to be creative with colour elsewhere, and will work with any scheme if you decide to redecorate. Traditional fittings

and taps suit the decorative mood of this room.

Tiles: Existing wall tiles can easily be painted, but you must first prepare the surface by applying tile primer or multi-surface primer. Follow this with a top coat of gloss in the colour of your choice, or use special tile paints. To freshen up the grout or restore its colour after painting, trace over it using a grout pen.

Window: Elaborate bathroom curtains can suffer splashes or get in the way of taps, but this more practical blind and pelmet combination offers an equally dressy alternative. While the ruched blind hangs neatly within the recess, the window is framed by a painted MDF pelmet, cut with curved corners and edged with upholstery piping. Lollipops, shells and fish ornaments glued on top complete this fun look.

BATHROOM TIP
Combining strong colours requires courage, but one way of checking out your ideas is by making a sample board. Glue paint shades, fabric swatches and other furnishing samples to a large sheet of card to get an idea of how they work together

The look: Bring an aura of old-fashioned romance to your ablutions. This look combines graceful lines and classic styling with homely touches, such as plants and pictures, for a comfortably lived-in feel.

Colour: A palette of airy colours evokes château-style elegance, with fresh cream and delicate eau-de-nil creating a light, feminine backdrop. The white suite and mirror surround stand out crisply against these soft colours, while the flowing transparent shower curtain emphasizes the mood of romance. The dark wood floorboards and furniture lend the room a more solidly traditional feel, and accents of red and terracotta in the soaps and tiles also strengthen the look.

Suite: The roll-top bath and generously sized basin have the classic appeal that's essential for this scheme, but it's the Victorian loo that catches the eye. With its floral base, and a high-level cistern surrounded by a rough wooden box, it adds to the air of vintage chic.

Mirror: An ornately carved surround turns a simple square mirror into a grand feature. Try making a similar surround by using plain timber to create a wide mirror frame, and then gluing on beading and decorative mouldings. When the entire surface is painted white, they will give a convincing panelled and carved effect.

Accessories: If you've space for one, a chair adds a feeling of comfort to a bathroom, and a padded seat cushion makes it look even cosier.

The look: Traditional details and distinctive accessories set within a smart but simple colour scheme give this bathroom and adjoining toilet a mood of understated elegance.

Colour: Smoky greys and soft neutrals make a sophisticated mix, while the wood tones of the door and bath surround add natural warmth. Instead of painting skirtings and architraves in white, choose a colour that complements the wall. The beige splashback tiles also blend comfortably with the lilac-toned walls, leaving the floor to liven things up with its chequerboard of pale and dark grey squares.

Suite: The fittings combine clean curves with classic detailing: the basin's elegant arched moulding is repeated in the loo cistern, and the loo seat matches the limed-oak-effect bath panelling. The etched design on the glass shower screen completes the traditional styling.

Floor: The floor design is painted on the diagonal, making the squares look like diamonds. Prepare sanded boards by applying knotting and wood primer or, if already painted or varnished, sand them to provide a key. Plan your design on graph paper before marking it on the floor. Mask off the paler squares first using low-tack tape, and fill in with two coats of floor paint. When dry, remove the tape and repeat for the darker squares. Finish with two coats of floor varnish.

Accessories: Just one unusual object can add character, and the arched mirror strikes a stylishly rustic note with its frame covered in twigs and driftwood. A collection of traditional accessories makes an interesting display above the loo. The shelf is decorated with a fancy edging, made simply by cutting fabric to shape using pinking shears. Secure it to the shelf with upholstery tacks.

BATHROOM TIP
If you have a large family, fitting your loo in a separate room will cut down on queues in the morning. Alternatively, you could try screening it from washing areas by building a partition wall to provide a measure of privacy

STOCKISTS:

SUITES AND TAPS

ANTIQUE BATHS OF IVYBRIDGE
Huge choice of restored period baths and sanitaryware.
Tel: 01752 698250

ARMITAGE SHANKS
Suites for every setting, from cottage-style to contemporary.
Tel: 0800 866 966
www.armitage-shanks.co.uk

ASTON MATTHEWS
Wide range of baths, from roll-top to hi-tech designs, plus basins, loos and bidets.
Tel: 020 7226 7220
www.astonmatthews.co.uk

AVILION
High-quality taps in chrome, gold, nickel and pewter finishes.
Tel: 01708 526361
www.avilion.co.uk

BATH DOCTOR
Restoration work carried out on antique baths and sanitaryware.
Tel: 01795 591711

BATHROOM CITY
Over 100 bathrooms on display.
Good cash and carry deals.
Tel: 0121 708 0111
www.bathroomcity.co.uk

BATHROOM DISCOUNT CENTRE
Discounts on famous-name bathroom fittings.
Tel: 020 7381 4222
www.bathroomdiscount.co.uk

BATHSTORE.COM
Wide range of sanitaryware, taps and showers to buy on-line.
Tel: 07000 228478
www.bathstore.com

BC SANITAN
Suites, taps and accessories in traditional period styles.
Tel: 01782 717175
www.jacuzzi.com

COLOURWASH
Contemporary designer-style fittings, including coloured glass and stainless steel basins.
Tel: 020 8947 5578
www.colourwash.co.uk

CP HART
High-quality suites and furniture, including up-to-the-minute looks by designer Philippe Starck.
Tel: 020 7902 1000
www.cphart.co.uk

DOLOMITE
Suites, fitted furniture and accessories in styles inspired by different periods or countries.
Tel: 0800 138 0922
www.dolomite-bathrooms.com

DOLPHIN BATHROOMS
Styles ranging from country cottage to city chic, some including furniture, with complete design and installation service.
Tel: 0800 626717
www.dolphinbathrooms.com

IDEAL-STANDARD
Wide range of contemporary and classic fittings, including suites designed to fit into small spaces.
Tel: 01482 499414
www.ideal-standard.co.uk

THE IMPERIAL BATHROOM CO
Traditional-style suites and storage furniture.
Tel: 01922 743074
www.imperial-bathrooms.co.uk

JACOB DELAFON
Stylish French suites and other fittings in a range of styles, from classic to ultra-modern.
Tel: 01235 510511

JACUZZI
Whirlpool baths in a range of shapes and sizes.
Tel: 01782 717175
www.jacuzzi.com

MAGNET
Modern and traditional suites, including roll-top and whirlpool baths; computer-aided planning. Branches nationwide.
www.magnet.co.uk

ROYAL DOULTON
High-quality suites and taps with distinctive contemporary looks.
Tel: 01270 879777

SHIRES BATHROOMS
Wide range of classic-style suites, taps and accessories.
Tel: 01274 521199
www.shires-bathrooms.co.uk

SOTTINI
Upmarket suites in contemporary and traditional designs, including sculptural wall-hung fittings and roll-top, whirlpool and spa baths.
Tel: 0800 591586
www.sottini.co.uk

STIFFKEY BATHROOMS
Traditional designs, including original sanitaryware and high-quality reproductions.
Tel: 01603 627850
www.stiffkeybathrooms.com

TWYFORD BATHROOMS
Wide range of modern, classic and Art Deco suites and taps at prices to suit every pocket.
Tel: 0870 840 1000
www.twyfordbathrooms.com

VERNON TUTBURY
Stylish contemporary sanitaryware and trendy accessories.
Tel: 01782 717175
www.jacuzzi.com

VILLEROY & BOCH
Basins and vanity units with innovative modern designs.
Tel: 020 8871 4028
www.villeroy-boch.com

VITRA
Contemporary designs, with a good choice of back-to-wall and wall-hung sanitaryware.
Tel: 01235 820400

THE WATER MONOPOLY
Fully restored antique sanitaryware from all periods.
Tel: 020 7624 2636
www.watermonopoly.com

SHOWERS

AQUALISA
High-performance electric, power and mixer showers.
Tel: 01959 560000
www.aqualisa.co.uk

DARYL SHOWERS
Multi-spray showers; enclosures, doors and bath screens in a variety of different finishes.
Tel: 0151 606 5000
www.daryl-showers.co.uk

HANSGROHE
Trendsetting designs, including the Pharo Shower Temple, an enclosure combining overhead, hand and body showers.
Tel: 01372 465655
www.hansgrohe.co.uk

HÜPPE
High-quality shower enclosures in stylish contemporary shapes; wide range of bath screens.
Tel: 01260 276188
www.hueppe.com

MATKI
Designer shower enclosures, shower trays and bath screens.
Tel: 01454 322888
www.matki.co.uk

MIRA SHOWERS
Wide range of electric, mixer and power showers.
Tel: 01242 221221
www.mira-showers.co.uk

SHOWERLUX
Wide range of shower enclosures, including some fitted with hydrotherapy jets; baths in some unusual shapes.
Tel: 024 7688 2515
www.duscholux.ch

TRITON
Wide range of electric, mixer and power showers at prices to suit all pockets.
Tel: 024 7637 2222
www.tritonshowers.co.uk

ACOVA RADIATORS
Heated towel rails, towel-drying radiators and tall radiators that incorporate mirrors.
Tel: 01562 753001
www.acova.co.uk

BISQUE RADIATORS
Designer-style radiators, including some unusual shapes, available in white and a wide range of colours.
Tel: 01225 478500
www.bisque.co.uk

DK HEATING SYSTEMS
Underfloor heating systems, towel warming units and fog-free backing to prevent mirrors from steaming up.
Tel: 020 8861 2844
www.dkheating.com

MHS RADIATORS
Traditional and modern radiator designs in various colours and finishes; heated towel rails.
Tel: 01268 591010
www.mhsradiators.co.uk

HEATING AND VENTILATION

MYSON TOWEL WARMERS
Towel warmers in many shapes, styles and sizes, including radiator models.
Tel: 01204 863200
www.mysontowelwarmers.co.uk

THE RADIATOR COMPANY
Stylish radiators in traditional and modern designs; towel warmers in various finishes.
Tel: 01342 302250
www.theradiatorcompany.co.uk

VASCO
Luxury bathroom radiators and heated towel rails.
Tel: 01933 278802
www.vasco.be

VENT-AXIA
Extractor fans and ventilation units designed for bathrooms.
Tel: 020 8549 2271
www.vent-axia.com

LIGHTING

BHS
Stylish but affordable lights and shades in a range of styles.
Tel: 020 7262 3288
www.bhs.co.uk

CHRISTOPHER WRAY LIGHTING
Huge range of light fittings, from traditional to cutting-edge.
Tel: 020 7736 8434
www.christopher-wray.com

HABITAT
Contemporary light fittings in chrome and glass.
Tel: 0845 601 0740
www.habitat.net

HOMEBASE
Wide range of fittings, including ceiling and eyeball lights.
Tel: 0870 900 8098
www.homebase.co.uk

JOHN CULLEN LIGHTING
Discreet modern lighting, such as spots and downlighters.
Tel: 020 7371 5400
www.johncullenlighting.co.uk

LONDON LIGHTING CO
Wide range of lighting, including downlighters, recessed spots and halogen lights.
Tel: 020 7589 3612

MR LIGHT
Stylish range of bathroom lighting, including unobtrusive halogen spotlights.
Tel: 020 7352 7525

RYNESS
Practical well-made fittings, including recessed eyeball ceiling lights, halogen spots and slimline striplights.
Tel: 020 7278 8993
www.ryness.co.uk

SKK LIGHTS
Innovative contemporary light fittings, including floor-mounted spotlights and minimalist-style back-lit panels.
Tel: 020 7434 4095
www.skk.net

FLOORING

ALLIED CARPETS
Carpet superstores with a huge range of colours and patterns.
Tel: 08000 932932

AMTICO
Quality vinyl flooring, including wood, stone and glass effects.
Tel: 0800 667766
www.amtico.com

CRUCIAL TRADING
Natural floorcoverings in sisal, coir and seagrass.
Tel: 01562 825656
www.crucial-trading.com

DALSOUPLE
Rubber flooring in many colours.
Tel: 01984 667233
www.dalsouple.com

FIRED EARTH
Marble, slate, terracotta and ceramic floor tiles, including Roman-style mosaic effects.
Tel: 01295 814300
www.firedearth.com

FORBO-NAIRN
Practical flooring, including natural product Marmoleum.
Tel: 01592 643777
www.nairn-cushionflor.co.uk

HARVEY MARIA
PVC laminated floor tiles with
funky photographic images.
Tel: 020 8516 7788
www.harveymaria.co.uk

KÄHRS FLOORING
Hardwood flooring, mostly from
sustainable Swedish forests.
Tel: 01243 778747
www.kahrs.se

RICHARD BURBIDGE
Easy-fit wood-laminate boards.
Tel: 01691 678201
www.richardburbidge.co.uk

WICANDERS
High-quality wood and cork
flooring in many finishes.
Tel: 01403 710001
www.wicanders.co.uk

SPLASHBACKS

BRAGMAN FLETT
All types of sheet metal, including copper, brass, aluminium and
stainless steel.
Tel: 020 8337 1934

CORRES MEXICAN TILES
Handmade terracotta tiles with
painted Mexican-style designs.
Tel: 020 7261 0941

DECORUM CERAMICS
Colourful plain and patterned
handpainted tiles.
Tel: 01494 882299
www.decorum-ceramics.co.uk

FIRED EARTH
Stylish wall tiles, including
handmade, mosaic and glass.
Tel: 01295 814300
www.firedearth.com

H&R JOHNSON CERAMICS
Good choice of tiles, including
country-style designs with a
handcrafted appearance.
Tel: 01782 575575
www.johnson-tiles.com

MOSAIC WORKSHOP
Wide range of mosaic tiles, plus
products needed to apply them.
Tel: 020 7263 2997
www.mosaicworkshop.com

PILKINGTON'S CERAMIC TILES
Huge selection of ceramic tiles
for both walls and floors.
Tel: 0161 727 1001
www.pilkingtons.com

THE REJECT TILE SHOP
Seconds and discontinued lines
at bargain prices.
Tel: 020 7731 6098
www.criterion-tiles.co.uk

THE TILE GALLERY
Reproduction Victorian and
Edwardian wall and floor tiles.
Tel: 020 7385 8818

COLOROLL
Contemporary wallcoverings.
Tel: 0800 056 4878
www.englewood.co.uk

CONTOUR
Wipe-clean vinyl wallpapers,
including tile and mosaic effects.
Tel: 01670 718300

CROWN PAINTS
Vast choice of shades, including
the Kitchen & Bathroom range.
Tel: 01254 704951
www.crownpaint.co.uk

**CROWN WALLCOVERINGS &
HOME FURNISHINGS**
Wide range of wallcoverings.
Tel: 0800 458 1554
www.ihdg.co.uk

WICKES
Tongue-and-groove boarding;
glass blocks for partition walls.
Tel: 0870 608 9001
www.wickes.co.uk

DULUX
Vast choice of shades, including
the Kitchens & Bathrooms
range.
Tel: 01753 550555
www.dulux.co.uk

HAMMERITE
Paints for use on metal surfaces.
Tel: 01661 830000
www.hammerite.com

HOMEBASE
Wide choice of shades, including Kitchen & Bathroom emul-
sions.
Tel: 0870 900 8098
www.homebase.co.uk

PAINTS AND WALLPAPERS

INTERNATIONAL PAINT
Paints and primers for tiles,
melamine, radiators and floors.
Tel: 01962 711177
www.international-paints.co.uk

PLASTI-KOTE
Spray paints, including metallics,
suitable for most surfaces.
Tel: 01223 836400
www.spraypaint.com

SANDERSON
Extensive paint and wallpaper
collections.
Tel: 01895 830000
www.sanderson-uk.com

DECORATIVE EFFECTS

BRANDON MARKETING
Kits for DIY bath resurfacing.
Tel: 01302 788138
www.brandonmarketing.co.uk

THE ENGLISH STAMP COMPANY
Wall stamps and stamping tools.
Tel: 01929 439117
www.englishstamp.com

HOMECRAFTS DIRECT
Wide range of craft products
available by mail order.
Tel: 0116 269 7733
www.homecrafts.co.uk

HUMBROL
Makers of Glass Etch spray that
simulates a frosted effect on
window and door panes.
Tel: 0800 132379

JALI
Decorative MDF shelf trims and
fretwork panels; radiator covers
made to measure.
Tel: 01227 831710
www.jali.co.uk

L CORNELISSEN & SON
Aluminium, silver and gold leaf,
plus tools for gilding.
Tel: 020 7636 1045
www.cornelissen.co.uk

THE PAINTED FINISH
Glazes, varnishes and tools for
creating paint effects.
Tel: 01926 842376
www.craftychick.com

RONSEAL

Paint & Grain kits for creating a woodgrain effect on flat surfaces; floor paints and wood-stains.
Tel: 0114 246 7171
www.ronseal.co.uk

ECLECTICS

Ready-made and made-to-measure roller and Roman blinds in smart modern designs.
Tel: 0870 010 2211
www.eclectics.co.uk

JOHN LEWIS

Blinds and curtains ready-made and made to order. Wide range of fabrics and window furniture such as poles and finials.
Tel: 020 7629 7711
www.johnlewis.co.uk

LUXAFLEX

Made-to-measure blinds in modern styles, including Venetian and pinoleum.
Tel: 08000 399399
www.luxaflex.com

STENCIL LIBRARY

Stencils and stencilling tools.
Tel: 01661 844844
www.stencil-library.com

NEXT HOME

Ready-made curtains and blinds, including Venetian, Roman, roller and bamboo designs.
Tel: 0870 243 5435 for stockists, 0845 600 7000 for mail order
www.next.co.uk

PRÊT À VIVRE

Curtains and blinds made to measure; poles and tiebacks.
Tel: 020 8960 6111
www.pretavivre.com

ROSEBYS

Ready-made curtains and blinds.
Tel: 0115 925 5999
www.rosebys.com

RUFFLETTE

Blind and eyelet kits; curtain tracks, rings and clips.
Tel: 0161 998 1811
www.rufflette.com

WINDOW TREATMENTS

THE SHUTTER SHOP
Wooden shutters made to order;
wooden Venetian blinds.
Tel: 01252 844575
www.shuttershop.co.uk

VELUX
Skylight windows and blinds
designed to fit them.
Tel: 0800 316 8822
www.velux.co.uk

STORAGE AND ACCESSORIES

AERO
Trendy accessories in pale
wood, chrome and plastic, many
by famous designers.
Tel: 020 8971 0022
www.aeroliving.com

CHRISTY
Wide range of towels, plus
coordinating bathmats.
Tel: 0161 368 1961
www.christy-towels.com

COLOGNE & COTTON
Luxurious towels and toiletries.
Tel: 01926 332573

THE COTSWOLD COMPANY
Storage furniture and baskets in
wood and woven fibres.
Tel: 01252 391404
www.cotswoldco.com

DAMASK
Pastel-coloured towels, prettily
packaged perfumes and painted
classic-style side tables.
Tel: 020 7731 3470
www.damask.co.uk

HABITAT
Contemporary storage accessories, including racks, shelving
and laundry baskets.
Tel: 0845 601 0740
www.habitat.net

HAF DESIGNS
Stainless steel wall-mounted
fittings, loo-brush holders and
door handles in sleek contemporary designs.
Tel: 01992 505655
www.hafdesigns.co.uk

THE HOLDING COMPANY
Contemporary storage furniture
and containers in wicker,
Perspex and chrome.
Tel: 020 7610 9160
www.theholdingcompany.co.uk

THE HAMBLEDON

Stylish accessories, including soapstone containers and a bamboo duckboard.
Tel: 01962 890055
www.housemailorder.co.uk

IKEA

Freestanding storage units and wall-mounted fittings in a range of finishes, from country pine to modern metal and glass.
Tel: 020 8208 5600
www.ikea.co.uk

MARKS & SPENCER

Towel and bathmat sets; baskets; ranges of wall-mounted fittings in beech, stainless steel, brass and glass.
Tel: 020 7935 4422 for stockists, 0845 603 1603 for mail order
www.marks-and-spencer.co.uk

MCCORD DESIGN BY MAIL

Willow and wicker storage baskets; chrome racks and rails.
Tel: 0870 908 7005
www.emccord.com

MUJI

Minimalist storage accessories made from cardboard, polypropylene and steel.
Tel: 020 7323 2208

NATURAL PRODUCTS

Toiletries, cosmetics and bathcare products.
Tel: 020 8735 2888
www.npw.co.uk

NEXT HOME

Varied accessory collections in materials ranging from chrome and glass to dark wood and rattan; towels in many colours.
Tel: 0870 243 5435 for stockists, 0845 600 7000 for mail order.
www.next.co.uk

OCEAN

Sleek contemporary storage and fittings, including metallic cabinets with frosted glass doors and simple steel wall fittings.
Tel: 08702 426283
www.oceancatalogue.com

OPAL LONDON

Stylish toiletries and bathcare ranges, including everything from brushes to bathrobes.
Tel: 020 8450 7834
www.opal-london.com

PURVES & PURVES

Contemporary accessories, ranging from designer-style fittings to colourful plastics.
Tel: 020 7580 8223
www.purves.co.uk

SAMUEL HEATH

High-quality solid brass wall fittings and accessories, most with classic designs, available in a variety of finishes.
Tel: 0121 772 2303
www.samuel-heath.com

SHAKER

Shaker-style wooden furniture, peg rails, oval storage boxes and folk-art accessories.
Tel: 020 7935 9461
www.shaker.co.uk

SHOWERAIL

A large range of shower curtains in many sizes, some with cartoon characters or wacky designs; transparent loo seats; bath accessories.
Tel: 01983 852565
www.showerail.com

TURNSTYLE DESIGNS

Ranges of wall-mounted accessories, plus decorative details such as door knobs, hooks and cord pulls.
Tel: 01271 325325
www.turnstyle-designs.com

UTOPIA

Fully fitted bathroom furniture in a range of styles and finishes, plus lighting and accessories.
Tel: 01902 406400
www.utopiagroup.com

WATER FRONT

Stylish but practical classic-style fittings made from solid brass and available in several finishes.
Tel: 01865 379218

WIDGET

Brightly coloured accessories, including rubber bathmats, funky shower curtains and bubbly resin plugs, door knobs and loo seats.
Tel: 020 7640 9290
www.fuzzybubbles.com

THE BATHROOM SHOWROOM ASSOCIATION

Can supply details of show-rooms listed among their members and free advice leaflets on shopping for a new bathroom.
Tel: 01782 747123
www.bathroom-association.org

THE BUILDING CENTRE

Building information and advice; DIY guides available to buy; free reference library.
Tel: 020 7692 6200
www.buildingcentre.co.uk

THE LIGHTING ASSOCIATION

Advice on buying light fittings; lists of suppliers and a free buyers' guide available.
Tel: 01952 290905

NATIONAL ASSOCIATION OF PLUMBING, HEATING AND MECHANICAL SERVICES CONTRACTORS

Supply lists of members and advice on plumbing and heating.
Tel: 024 7647 0626
www.licensedplumber.co.uk

NATIONAL INSPECTION COUNCIL FOR ELECTRICAL INSTALLATION CONTRACTING

Can supply lists of electricians, free leaflets and advice on lighting and electrical matters.
Tel: 020 7564 2323

NATIONAL INSTITUTE OF CARPET AND FLOOR LAYERS

Help with finding the right professionals to fit flooring.
Tel: 0115 958 3077
www.nicltd.org.uk

SALVO

Nationwide list of salvage yards available for a small fee.
Tel: 01890 820333
www.salvo.co.uk

TILE ASSOCIATION

Can supply lists of tilers and advice on how to choose and care for ceramic tiles.
Tel: 020 8663 1569